Dr Pepper

KING OF BEVERAGES

by Harry E. Ellis

Centennial Edition

I.S.B.N. 0-9607448-1-9
Library of Congress Catalog Card No. 86-60338

Printed by Hart Graphics
Austin, Texas/Dallas, Texas

We commit to memory only
vaguely details of the past.
Were it not for the written
word, history would soon fade
into oblivion and demand that
lessons be learned over and
over!

—H. Ellis

CONTENTS

DEDICATION   6

1. CELEBRATING 100 ORIGINAL YEARS   8

2. COMPANY PRESIDENTS   11

3. 1980 – DR PEPPER LAUNCHES THE 80'S   15

4. 1981 – ADDING NEW DIMENSIONS   18

5. 1982 – NEW HORIZONS   21

6. 1983 – SPECIAL PROMOTIONS   25

7. 1984 – AN OUT-OF-THE-ORDINARY YEAR   29

8. 1985 – 100 ORIGINAL YEARS   35

9. FOUNDERS – ALDERTON, MORRISON, LAZENBY   43

10. LAZENBY'S LIQUID SUNSHINE   47

11. DR PEPPER ADVERTISING – OBJECT d'ART   48

12. MEET ME IN ST. LOUIE, LOUIE   58

13. DR PEPPER – KING OF BEVERAGES   63

14. THE MAN WHO PUT THE "POP" IN SODA POP   66

15. DRINK A BITE TO EAT AT 10-2 AND 4 O'CLOCK   70

16. SHOOT A WACO   73

17. ARTESIA BOTTLING COMPANY   78

18. DR PEPPER PACKAGING PARADE   84

19. '85 WAS A VERY GOOD YEAR   88

20. DR PEPPER FOUNDERS IN PERPETUITY   94

CREDIT AND ACKNOWLEDGEMENTS   96

*The history of a company
reflects the quality of its product,
the character of its people and
the total purpose for its existence*

— W.W.C.

Dedication

This Centennial edition of Dr Pepper history is, for many appropriate reasons, dedicated to W. W. "Foots" Clements, Chairman of the Board, CEO and fifty year salesman/administrator for the Company. Thanks to him the 100 year history of Dr Pepper is now published in this and an earlier edition completed in 1980 which, likewise, was dedicated to W.W. "Foots" Clements.

Among the leaders of the Company since Dr Pepper's origin in 1885, Mr. Clements has served as an executive officer longer than any. He has received many high honors and wide national recognition for himself and for Dr Pepper.

Starting out as a salesman for the Dr Pepper Bottling Co., of Tuscaloosa, Alabama in 1935, he established credentials which would lead him to outstanding sales and marketing achievements. In 1942 he joined the Dr Pepper Company as zone sales manager working with

bottlers in Virginia, North Carolina, West Virginia and Pennsylvania.

From there he went on to become sales promotion manager in 1944, general sales manager in 1948 and from 1951 to 1957 served as vice president-marketing. He was elected executive vice president and a director of the Company in January 1967.

His next move up the Dr Pepper corporate ladder was in March 1969, when he became president and chief operating officer, and a year later was elevated to chief executive officer. From March 1974 to February 1980 he was Chairman of the Board, President and CEO. He now serves as Chairman of the Board and CEO.

Throughout his career, beginning as early as the '40's, Clements has been involved in executive marketing decisions and a member of the Company's policy-making group. He became a catalyst for the Company's significant growth through the '60's and '70's. An inveterate sales-man, his two-pronged objective of building a solid sales-marketing organization and the industry's strongest bottler network resulted in Dr Pepper's rise from that of a "Texas drink" to one of significant national stature with great international potential.

Outside the Company he has held prestigious positions with many leading civic and business organizations including the National Alliance of Businessmen, Laymen's National Committee, American Red Cross, Salvation Army, United Fund, Inc., U.S.O., Boy Scouts of America and some forty business groups and institutions which he has served as director. He is a member of the executive board of three leading universities, Baylor, Southern Methodist and his alma mater, the University of Alabama.

Honors which have come to Mr. Clements include "Distinguished Sales and Marketing Executive of the Southwest," 1969; "The Golden Plate Award" from the American Academy of Achievement, 1970; "Marketing Man of the Decade" 1960-1970, from the North Texas Chapter, American Marketing Association; "Distinguished Salesman Award" 1972 from Sales and Marketing Executives of Dallas. He served as general chairman in 1973 of the Dallas Salute to Vietnam Veterans; was awarded Honorary Doctor of Humane Letters degree from the University of Alabama in 1975 and was recipient of the George Washington Certificate Award from the Freedom Foundation at Valley Forge. In 1975 he was named "Entrepreneur of the Year" by the Southern Methodist University School of Business and in 1976 the "Beverage Industry Man of the Year" by Beverage Industry Magazine.

He was honored as "Chief Executive Officer of the Year — Beverage Industry" by Financial World Magazine in 1977 and in 1978, Sales and Marketing Executives International presented him with their "Statesman of the Year" award. In 1980 he received the "Horatio Alger Award"; in 1980 also the "Distinguished American Award" from the Lone Star Chapter of the National Football Foundation Hall of Fame,

Inc; and in 1982 was named to the Beverage World Hall of Fame.

In 1968 Mr. Clements became a director and president of the Sales and Marketing Executives, International and in 1969-70 was chairman of the board. He is past president of the Dallas Sales and Marketing Executives. The list of titles and honors that have come to Mr. Clements is indicative of the leadership he has provided not only to his own profession but to many worthy institutions as well.

There are special qualities not specifically mentioned about Mr. Clements which reflect his nature and character. He places high priority on human relations, makes friends with most of whom he meets. In his climb to the top his policy was to take others up the ladder with him but never climbing too high to forget or overlook those he met along the way.

He is a stickler for sticking to basic fundamentals but always ready to move beyond new horizons. He urges others to dream big dreams and believe they can become real.

The crowning mark of W. W. Clements throughout his career with Dr Pepper was that of a "salesman" — always closing a sale with "Thanks for your Dr Pepper business."

It is therefore with gratitude that we dedicate this second edition of Dr Pepper history to W. W. "Foots" Clements and say . . . *"Thanks for your Dr Pepper business which has made history for Dr Pepper so successful for fifty years!"*

"Thanks for your
Dr Pepper Business!"

CELEBRATING

Original Years

This is a five-year update of the corporate history of Dr Pepper Company published in 1980 in a book titled "Dr Pepper - King of Beverages." The original history was a 95-year documentary of the Company beginning with the origin of Dr Pepper at Morrison's Old Corner Drug in Waco, Texas in 1885.

With this writing we thus complete the history of the Company's One Hundred Original Years; appropriate to the observance of its Centennial Celebration.

There is some redundancy with the first edition and with good reason. It allows those who have not read the original story to capture some of the excitement of Dr Pepper's colorful past. Even though some of the record is a repeat, it is published here in anecdote with new and interesting details uncovered since the original edition appeared. The story of Dr Pepper becomes more remarkable as it unfolds.

The author is twice honored to have the opportunity to compile both editions which comprise an out-of-the-ordinary story about an out-of-the-ordinary product.

Out-of-the-ordinary is simply another way to describe many unique things about Dr Pepper. It started out as a uniquely different and distinctively flavored soft drink, a quality that became its greatest asset and remains so one hundred years since its origin.

The story of Dr Pepper, as told in "Dr Pepper - King of Beverages," is a chronological account of how the Company has capitalized on this distinctive flavor. As significant as its flavor is the fact that Dr Pepper can be enjoyed by consumers day in and day out without tiring of its taste; possible only to a few other carbonated drinks.

Another exclusive feature about Dr Pepper, not discovered until 1958, is that it can be enjoyed as a hot beverage.

These and other illuminating facts about the product are fully documented in the first edition. For the record, we resume here the corporate story of Dr Pepper in 1981 to complete the centennial period ending in 1985 and to commemorate Dr Pepper's 100 Original Years.

On reading the history of Dr Pepper it becomes easy to feel we are a part of it and that history is still being made. As interesting as the word picture are the graphics which illustrate the wide variety of advertising and promotional tools used in promoting the sale of Dr Pepper. Not only do they mark various time frames in which they were used, they also reflect the ideas of those engaged in the sale of the drink.

The accuracy of history involves more than research, however patient and penetrating. The narrator must become, as it were, a spectator of that about which he writes. By that reason, the author stakes claim to the bona fide nature of this and the previous historical edition as well.

There are special reasons for this supplementary edition other than to mark the Company's centennial celebration. The five-year period, '81–'85, has been witness to events which are entirely new to the Company's previous history and promises great impact on its future.

Drawing attention to Dr Pepper's Centennial year, Dr Pepper cans in many bottler markets carried early vintage art and vignettes of its past. In limited number these cans immediately became popular as "collectibles."

While the first edition served to prologize Dr Pepper's past, this second edition updates the Dr Pepper story and reestablishes interesting facts about the product, its strength and potential.

Dr Pepper, like every other soft drink, experienced radical changes in business ideologies. History will show that all American business enterprise during the period '81 through '85 was introduced to a revolution of new ideas, methods and procedures never experienced before. Many long-standing traditions disappeared; radical new policies were introduced that changed the business climate for all soft drink bottlers. Companies with enviable heritage found themselves in the hands of new managers who were not bound by traditions of the past. Some had no qualms in abandoning policies which had formed the character and nature of the business and brought it great success.

In light of these circumstances, it is an understatement that the five-year period here recorded brought unprecedented changes not only for Dr Pepper but for all soft drink brands as well.

It has often been said and bears repeating that Dr Pepper occupies a unique position in the soft drink industry. Its early founders, and many who have been closely associated with Dr Pepper over the years, were convinced that its unique flavor and its ability to satisfy taste would earn it a place in the sun among all other carbonated brands. It ranks number 4 in its industry, which has reached a stage of competitiveness greater than at any time in its history.

Based on Dr Pepper's performance over its One Hundred Original Years, the best evidence of its success is the figures that follow. It began its major thrust in the thirties and the figures tell its growth story.

YEAR	NET SALES	NET PROFITS
1920	$ 152,515.73	$ 2,564.64
1930	1,531,719.46	387,329.46
1940	3,399,792.69	731,187.41
1950	6,839,210.33	604,810.05
1960	13,308,488.00	626,531.00
1970	57,449,749.00	5,629,021.00
1980	333,165,320.00	26,543,054.00

It is noteworthy that in some years Dr Pepper progressed at a rate of two and three times that of the industry. During the five-year period, '81–'85, however, Dr Pepper experienced a number of reverses, some of its own making. There was only limited support in certain areas, neglect in others and it was victim of some unsound judgment. In some cases, it was suppressed by franchised bottlers where its competitive sting was being felt by some of their other brands.

In spite of a depressed economy, the stiffened competition and self-inflicted mistakes, Dr Pepper continues to demonstrate its strength and, as its centennial period ends, heads into its second 100 years on a positive note. And what could be more positive than the Company's record sales in its Centennial year, the greatest in its 100 year history!

COMPANY PRESIDENTS
1980-1985

A biographical record of the men who served as president of Dr Pepper Company from the time of its founding in 1923 through 1980 was published in a corporate history in 1980 under the title "Dr Pepper — King of Beverages." To complete the one hundred year history of Dr Pepper (1885–1985) it becomes relevant for the record to include those who have served during the ensuing five-year period.

In looking at these dates, it is essential to remember that the drink Dr Pepper originated in Waco, Texas in 1885 and that prior to 1923, the Company had operated first as The Circle "A" Corporation of America and later as The Artesian Manufacturing and Bottling Company.

During that period, Robert S. Lazenby had been the principal figure serving as president of these two respective companies. Since the founding of the present company in 1923, the following men have occupied the office of president:

R. S. Lazenby	1907-1923
O. S. Carlton	1923-1926
J. W. Link	1927-1933
J. B. O'Hara	1934-1943
D. C. Bryan	1943-1949
L. M. Green	1950-1958
W. R. Parker	1958-1967
H. S. Billingsley	1967-1969
W. W. Clements	1969-1980
C. L. Jarvie	1980-1982
R. Q. Armstrong	1982-1984
J. K. Hughes	1984
J. R. Albers	1984-

Charles L. Jarvie

Richard Q. Armstrong

CHARLES L. JARVIE

C. L. Jarvie became the tenth president of Dr Pepper Company on February 26, 1980, succeeding W. W. Clements who had held the post since 1969. Jarvie, 43, a graduate of Cornell University, was a relative newcomer to the soft drink business, having served twenty years in sales and management positions with Procter & Gamble. He brought with him to Dr Pepper excellent credentials in sales, marketing and general management. His selection as president ended a lengthy search by the Company for executive leadership.

Jarvie was energetic, enthusiastic and a man on the move. He introduced a number of new programs to Dr Pepper which, under other circumstances, could well have ignited the Company's operations. A cardinal difference for Jarvie was to assume that selling soft drinks was the same as selling soap products. There was a great difference, particularly in the areas of distribution and marketing.

Dr Pepper had built its business over a long period through cooperative effort with its network of franchised bottlers who are totally autonomous in the operation of their legally designated markets. The Company places high priority on its bottler relations, regarded among the best in the soft drink industry. Jarvie saw the priority to be in the development of national accounts and centered much of the Company's marketing efforts in that direction.

It brought increased volume among national accounts but not enough to offset the sharp decline in bottler sales. The result was a severe loss in Dr Pepper's overall market share.

Jarvie's aggressive, hard-driving style contrasted too sharply with the Company's long established procedures. His view and strategy were simply too radically different from those which had guided Dr Pepper to become the number three soft drink among the nation's leading brands.

He tendered his resignation as president of the Company in November 1982.

RICHARD Q. ARMSTRONG

Stepping into the presidency of Dr Pepper Company on November 24, 1982 was Richard Q. Armstrong, 46, replacing C. L. Jarvie who had resigned. With eight years of management experience in the soft drink industry, Armstrong was well grounded in the fundamentals of the job.

A native of Boston and an honors graduate of Bowdoin College in Brunswick, Maine, he had worked thirteen years in senior account positions at major advertising agencies including Ted Bates, Benton and Bowles and Needham, Harper and Steers.

He left the agency business to become vice president and director of marketing for Dobbs-Life Savers International, a unit of Squibb.

In 1976, Armstrong joined Canada Dry as president of its international division and in 1979 became president and chief operating officer for the company. He was credited with a dramatic turnaround of Canada Dry's domestic operations due largely to a management team which he had assembled.

On February 2, 1982, Dr Pepper acquired from Norton Simon, Inc., the Canada Dry Corporation where Armstrong was serving as president and chief executive officer.

Thus he was already associated with Dr Pepper and the logical man to step into the presidency, continuing also as president of Canada Dry.

Armstrong served as president of Dr Pepper Company until February 28, 1984 at which time stockholders voted to approve a tender offer from Forstmann Little & Co., for the purchase of all outstanding shares of stock in the Company. A long-time resident of New England, he elected to return there to pursue previously established career goals.

He became the eleventh and last president of Dr Pepper Company as a public corporation.

JOE K. HUGHES

Joe K. Hughes

On March 6, 1984, Joe K. Hughes became the twelfth president of Dr Pepper Company and the first to occupy the post under its new ownership which became effective February 28, 1984. The Company, on that date, entered into a merger agreement with Forstmann Little & Co., a New York investment firm, following approval of the Company's stockholders to accept $22 per share for their holdings.

Hughes, 56, ascended to the post as president and chief operating officer after sixteen years with the Company. His affiliation with Dr Pepper, however, dates back to 1954 when he became associated with Harshe Rotman, Inc., a Chicago public relations firm, as manager of their Dallas office where he was assigned to the Dr Pepper account.

He resigned his position with Harshe Rotman in 1956 to join Grant Advertising, Inc., as manager of their Dallas office and to serve as account manager on the Dr Pepper account. In 1958, he was named president-manager of Grant's Dallas office and became executive vice president and supervisor on the Dr Pepper account.

In 1968, Hughes joined Dr Pepper Company as vice president-franchising; in 1969 became vice president-marketing services; elected vice president-marketing in 1970 and executive vice president in 1973.

Hughes also served as a director for five of the Company's corporate-owned bottling companies and Dr Pepper Japan Company.

A native Texan and a graduate of Southern Methodist University in Dallas, Hughes began his career working as an editor for the *Dallas Times Herald*. His thirty years of experience with Dr Pepper in public relations, advertising and marketing gave him a broad knowledge of the Company which earned him the presidency.

John R. Albers

JOHN R. ALBERS

Thirteenth president and chief operating officer of Dr Pepper Company is John R. Albers, elected to the post on December 3, 1984. He succeeded Joe K. Hughes who was named as vice chairman of the Company.

Albers is a native of Minneapolis where he received his early schooling and attended the University of Minnesota. His studies were interrupted by two years of military service in the U.S. Army where he ranked as a 1st lieutenant. He returned to the university, graduating in 1957 with a B.A. Degree in Economics and did post graduate work at Stanford University in Stanford, California.

Like most of his predecessors at Dr Pepper, Albers' background was in advertising and marketing. He began his career in 1959 with Campbell-Mithun Advertising, where he served as account executive on the Pillsbury account. In 1964 he joined Grant Advertising in Dallas as a vice president and account executive for Dr Pepper and Burrus Mills. He returned to Minneapolis in 1965 as account supervisor for Knox-Reeves on the General Mills, Pillsbury and Alberto-Culver accounts.

In 1969 Albers co-founded Zapata International, a Mexican food franchise restaurant chain. He served as director and chairman/secretary/treasurer until joining Dr Pepper Company on May 1, 1971 as vice president-advertising. In 1974 he was named vice president-marketing and in September 1980 was elected senior vice president-marketing.

In 1982 Albers left Dr Pepper for a brief period to manage a venture capital firm and returned in May 1983 as president-Dr Pepper USA, heading up the Company's domestic sales-marketing unit. He was responsible for elements providing sales and marketing support to some 450 licensed Dr Pepper bottlers in the U.S., including advertising, promotions, and a national field organization of sales representatives assisting bottlers with take-home, cold bottle and fountain/foodservice sales of Dr Pepper, Sugar Free Dr Pepper, Pepper Free and Sugar Free-Pepper Free drinks.

In March 1984 Albers moved up to corporate executive vice president with all major Company divisions reporting to his office, including domestic and international sales, manufacturing, finance and corporate-owned bottling plants.

An important qualification of Albers is his recognition and respect for the franchise bottler role in Dr Pepper progress.

Dr Pepper Launches The '80's _____

Dr Pepper started the eighties on a high note. On February 1, the Company announced as one of its marketing objectives the "Pepperization of America" and a continuation for the third year of the "Be A Pepper" campaign. In only two years this upbeat approach had become the third most popular advertising campaign in the U.S.

Millions of Americans were responding to the phrase, "Wouldn't you like to be a Pepper, too?" as sung by Dr Pepper's "Pied Pepper," David Naughton, as well as such recording artists as Michael Jackson and The Jacksons, Chic, The Statler Brothers, Tanya Tucker and The Little River Band. The latter group captured the IBA award as the best 60 second radio musical of the year.

Based on Dr Pepper's rapidly growing market share, these programs presented foreseeable goals for the Company; leading off the year was a nationwide promotion with retailing giant, J. C. Penney.

Award winning TV and radio commercials for the "I'm a Pepper" campaign had been impressively effective and some 1,800 Penney stores tied into it by offering a variety of sportswear and accessories featuring the slogan. May was declared "Be a Pepper Month" resulting in a highly successful promotion for both J. C. Penney and Dr Pepper.

Another important move on February 5 was the formation of

David Naughton, Dr Pepper's "Pied Pepper" was dancing and singing . . .
"I'm a Pepper, we're a Pepper, wouldn't you like to be a Pepper too?"

Dr Pepper Company/Canada to further expand Dr Pepper development in Canadian provinces.

Favorable volume growth and a sharp increase in the number of franchised bottlers prompted .the move. Headquarters for the newly-formed company were based in Toronto, staffed by twelve marketing and field sales people.

Dr Pepper had been available in Canada since 1961 when it was introduced in Windsor. Currently, there were twenty-eight franchised Dr Pepper bottlers serving approximately 55% of the Canadian market.

On February 26, the Company announced that Charles L. Jarvie, a 20-year veteran with Procter & Gamble, was joining Dr Pepper as president and chief operating officer. Jarvie's background had been in sales and marketing, including management of numerous P&G consumer services. At 43, he was the youngest to become president of the Company.

At the Company's annual stockholders meeting in Dallas on April 15, W. W. Clements, Chairman of the Board, announced that Dr Pepper had just become the number three soft drink in sales nationally.

In mid-May of 1980, the Company made a bid to acquire Crush International which proved unsuccessful, being outbid for the company by Procter & Gamble.

A number of special events were scheduled in 1980 to celebrate Dr Pepper's 95th birthday. One was a tie-in honoring all-time NFL passing great, Roger Staubach, who was retiring after ten years with the Dallas Cowboys. To mark the occasion, Dr Pepper produced a commemorative bottle which was formally presented to Staubach in special ceremonies at Texas Stadium in Dallas.

Another special event, co-sponsored by Dr Pepper and its New York City franchisee, The Coca-Cola Bottling Co. of New York, was the annual series of Mid-Summer Concerts in the Park from July 1 through August 30. Thirty-eight featured entertainers performed in the shows including Jefferson Starship, Judy Collins, Devo, Kenny Loggins, B. B. King and Melissa Manchester, to name a few.

Summertime promotions on Dr Pepper were in full swing elsewhere around the country. In the capital city of Austin, Texas, the Company and its bottlers jointly sponsored the 1980 National Tournament of Junior Golfers, under the auspices of the American Junior Golf Association. Top young golfers from every state in the nation competed in the event.

In Yakima, Washington, Dr Pepper was a patron at the finals of the National High School Rodeo Association held July 28 – August 3. More than 1,200 entrants from 33 states and two Canadian provinces competed in the events viewed by nearly 70,000 spectators. Dr Pepper visibility throughout the performances was high as were sales of the product.

Canadian bottlers in Orillia, Chatham and Essex, Ontario and in Owen Sound sponsored Dr Pepper promotions at a series of summer sports events including skiing, river raft races, bowling and soccer.

Mike Douglas, popular emcee of his own syndicated TV show, chose Dr Pepper's Old Corner Drug Store in Dallas as the scene for a segment of one of his shows. Joining him for the taping was David Naughton, Pied Pepper and star of Dr Pepper's TV commercials.

Thirty-two ounce commemorative bottle honoring NFL passing great Roger Staubach, used in Dr Pepper's 95th birthday celebration.

An August event sponsored by the Dr Pepper Bottling Co. of Minneapolis-St. Paul was the Patty Berg Women's Golf Classic.

Dr Pepper TV network specials in 1980 offered some of the nation's leading entertainers featuring such stars as Barry Manilow, Olivia Newton-John, Mac Davis, Ambrosia, Billy Preston and Syreeta and the Charlie Daniels Band.

TV commercials also captured the network spotlight with spirited singer-dancer David Naughton and Mickey Rooney doing a whistling performance.

The year 1980 brought some legislative actions that favored both Dr Pepper and the soft drink industry. A nine-year struggle with the Federal Trade Commission to preserve the integrity of the bottler franchise system reached a successful conclusion in July, when President Carter signed into law the Soft Drink Interbrand Competition Act. This law ensured preservation of the competitive franchise system of free enterprise.

On the international scene, and far removed from Texas, Dr Pepper was making new inroads, expanding its distribution into several new foreign markets. In October, the company announced new franchises in Sweden and Nigeria, the first ventures for Dr Pepper in Scandinavia and Africa. Over 1,100 attended the formal opening of a newly franchised bottling operation in Eket, Cross River State, Nigeria, on December 6, located in the lush tropical rain forest of West Africa.

Since entering Japan in 1974, the Company had franchised bottlers and distributors in Malta, Jordan, Saudi Arabia, Northern Ireland, Bermuda and Guatemala.

Dr Pepper Company selected San Francisco for its annual bottler meeting on October 6–7 to review marketing plans titled "Pepperization of America." One of the opening announcements at the meeting was the approval of the use of high fructose corn syrup 55 at 100% level as an alternative sweetner for Dr Pepper flavoring syrup.

One of the host speakers at the meeting was Dick Clark, veteran participant in Dr Pepper programs as far back as 1960. As always, the highlight of the meeting was the presentation of advertising for the coming year and the new themes it would offer. Sugar Free Dr Pepper, it was announced, would get major billing using a series of poster lines discounting its fattening effect. One poster tagline read "It tastes fattening, but it's not!"

Following the San Francisco meeting, representatives from 83 Dr Pepper bottling plants, winners in the Company's 1980 Travel Incentive Program, enjoyed a nine-day holiday in Switzerland. Their adventure began in Lucerne, followed by visits to the Bernese Alps, Montreaux and ending up in Zurich, largest Swiss city and industrial center.

Final event of the year was the National Soft Drink Association convention held in Chicago on November 10–12. It was the 62nd annual meeting of bottlers and drew near-record attendance of 13,200. Theme of the meeting was "It's People," with such dignitaries heading the program as President Gerald R. Ford, Dr. Henry Kissinger, Secretary of State and economist Dr. Herbert Stein.

It was a highlight convention for Dr Pepper as the chairman's gavel passed from one Dr Pepper bottler to another; Bill Roberson of Washington, N.C. turning the reins over to Norman Sisisky of Petersburg, Virginia.

Top honors for highest per capita Dr Pepper sales in 1980 went to the Dr Pepper Bottling Company, Crockett, Texas, marking the second year in a row for the bottler to receive the award.

1980 marked the 23rd consecutive year of sales and earnings increases for the Company. Net sales hit a new all-time high of $333,165,000, an increase of 14%, and earnings were $25,543,000, up 12% over 1979.

Heading into 1981 the Company was set for another round of tailored marketing programs for each of its 478 franchised markets. Launching its new ad campaign was the familiar and still popular theme, "Be a Pepper" which had generated record consumer shares for the product.

1981 "Adding New Dimensions" _____

The start of each new year for Dr Pepper is accented by two major national events taking place on January 1; its float participation in the annual Tournament of Roses Parade in Pasadena, and the Cotton Bowl Parade in Dallas; each seen on national television by millions of viewers. On January 1, 1981 the Company added two more parade winning trophies to its long gallery of float awards.

Dr Pepper marketing strategy going into 1981 took on several new dimensions. In January the Company arranged a $110 million credit facility with four major banks to provide greater financial flexibility for further expansion of the business as steady growth in the year ending pointed to new opportunities.

The continuing search for product improvements produced a new sweetener for Dr Pepper which was introduced on April 6. Dr Pepper Company was the first major soft drink manufacturer to conduct research on the use of high fructose corn syrup, and authorized its use by bottlers as a total sweetener for Dr Pepper. Earlier, in 1975, it had been approved as a 50% replacement for sucrose, the traditional soft drink sweetener.

The role of corporate bottling plants was attractive, and between April and October, Dr Pepper Company acquired operations in Pensacola, Florida; Mobile, Alabama and Albuquerque, New Mexico. Its Houston, Texas plant was moved into a new $20 million dollar production facility to keep pace with this fastest-growing Metroplex market in the United States.

Growth in the International Market in 1981 also continued with Dr Pepper being introduced by licensed bottlers and distributors in Chile, Pakistan and Syria. Establecimientos Nobis, based in Santiago, became the first Dr Pepper bottling operation in South America.

An early year promotion took place in February when skiers in the Pennsylvania area competed in a Dr Pepper sponsored race at Camelback in the Poconos. Dr Pepper bottlers in Wilmington, Delaware, and in Scranton, Philadelphia, Pottsville, Coatsville and Williamsport, Pennsylvania teamed up to promote the event.

The leading major promotion in a bottler option "Summer Surge" series was a repeat of the "Be A Pepper" tie-in with J. C. Penney stores. For the second year, more than 1,800 stores were involved in building displays and serving as redemption centers for consumers with winning under-the-crown "Pepper Prizes."

The "Summer Surge" program, opening in May and closing in October, offered a series of promotions including "Be A Pepper," "Buy Three and Get One Free," "Back to School," "Prize Sweepstakes," "Summer Cooler" and "Pepper Pigskin."

An important series of mid-year bottler meetings were held in April where the company fully apprised bottlers of the application and use of newly authorized High Fructose Corn Syrup as a total sweetener for Dr Pepper; also to review Dr Pepper promotional programs for the year.

The "Be A Pepper" theme captured the imagination of thousands of people who identified themselves as "Peppers" in a wide array of wearables, thanks to the excellent merchandising of the Penney stores across the country. May was designated "Be A Pepper Month" and proved to be an attention getter for Dr Pepper. The campaign was highlighted on TV, radio, outdoor and in print. One commercial was especially unique in that it contained no words, featuring that long popular and loveable character, Mickey Rooney, and David Naughton whistling the famous Pepper jingle. It proved to be another Dr Pepper winner when it was selected by Ad Age as one of the top commericals of the year.

Highlighting the "Be A Pepper" promotion was a national sweepstakes offering ten AMC Pepper-identified Jeeps as prizes.

At a reconvention of Dr Pepper Company stockholders on May 22, approval was made authorizing 4,000,000 shares of preferred stock, thus providing additional revenue for expanding the Company's business, for additional capital improvements and new acquisitions.

A major change in Dr Pepper and Sugar Free Dr Pepper logo graphics was introduced at mid-summer, adding color and brilliance. They were bold, big and impressive, particularly on vendors and delivery vehicles.

During the summer, several enterprising bottlers engaged in dramatic competition to build "The world's largest Dr Pepper display." Records were set in numerous markets including Oklahoma City, Oklahoma; Fort Smith and Paragould, Arkansas; and Roanoke, Virginia where displays appeared ranging in size from 2,000 to 23,000 cases.

"Be A Pepper" advertising had worked well since its inception in 1977, and in 1981, ranked among the top ten TV commercials of all consumer products according to the annual survey conducted by Video StoryBoards, Inc. Dr Pepper finished second in the survey ahead of all other soft drink brands and second only to Miller Lite beer.

Sugar Free Dr Pepper was moving in a fast lane for the Company with significant gains over a long period, accounting for nearly 20% of total sales.

To stimulate new interest, Sugar Free advertising was given a new themeline stressing both taste and challenge — "Oh, what a surprise, the taste will open your eyes." Another intriguing tag line on 1981 Sugar Free posters was, "It tastes fattening, but it's not." Media use for the product was expanded to include national magazines in an attempt to reach that elusive working woman; but it was also directed toward men, a minority group that had grown to represent 30% of the diet soft drink market. The message to both groups continued to emphasize the Sugar Free Dr Pepper taste. The national campaign, centering on the great taste of Sugar

Free Dr Pepper, captured a lot of consumer attention from a commercial featuring one of the hottest young singers on the air, Barbara Mandrell, who was named "Country Entertainer of the Year."

Dr Pepper radio commercials presented two popular musical groups, "Alabama" — judged Group of the Year by the Academy of Country Music, and "Air Supply" — Australia's latest entry on the pop music scene.

TV specials via the popular music route and under Dr Pepper sponsorship included the 16th Annual Academy of Country Music Awards in April, American Bandstand's 30th Anniversary show in October, and Dr Pepper's annual New Year's Rockin' Eve.

A signal honor came to George Kalil, Dr Pepper bottler in Tucson, Arizona during the year, when he was named "Arizona Small Business Man of the Year." The award is presented annually by the U.S. Small Business Administration Council. Kalil's company, founded in 1947, had gross sales in 1980 of more than $13 million.

Dr Pepper sales and distribution were reaching into new strategic areas served by the U.S. Military. On July 1, the Company appointed Mil-Brands, Inc., as its military representative for the Mediterranean area, including Turkey, Greece, Italy and the Middle East. Both Dr Pepper and Sugar Free Dr Pepper were available to U.S. Services personnel.

On September 1, Dr Pepper Company announced it had acquired a license to manufacture and market Welch's carbonated soft drinks in the United States. Welch Foods, Inc., the leading producer of U.S. grape products, was marketing its flavors through a network of 226 licensed bottlers. It was an important acquisition for the Company — opening up new channels of distribution for both Dr Pepper and Welch flavors.

The Welch's acquisition gave Dr Pepper Company a prestigious line of products. They were developed by the producers of Welch's Grape Juice, first introduced in 1869 by Dr. Thomas B. Welch, a New Jersey dentist who applied the theory used by Louis Pasteur in processing grapes to produce an unfermented wine that could be used in his church's communion service.

Like many other companies, Welch's expanded its line to other products including a variety of non-carbonated drinks. Five flavors are produced under the Welch's label and marketed by Dr

Pepper Company through Premier Beverages, a wholly-owned subsidiary.

October is traditionally an important month for Dr Pepper when the Company and its franchised bottlers meet to view upcoming advertising and marketing plans for the coming year. The 1981 meeting was held in Dallas October 4–6, where it was announced that within the category of Pepper type drinks, Dr Pepper alone accounted for 92 percent of total sales.

Closely following Dr Pepper's annual bottler meeting was the 1981 NSDA Annual Meeting and International Soft Drink Industry Exposition in Los Angeles, attended by some 9,000 bottlers. Again Beverage Industry Magazine honored a Dr Pepper bottler with its distinguished "Man of the Year" award, naming Phil Hughes, president of BPC of Tulsa which operates the Dr Pepper franchise for that market.

It was also an Oklahoma bottler who captured Dr Pepper's Top Per Capita Award for 1981, the Dr Pepper Bottling Company of Elk City being named the winner.

The final line on Dr Pepper operations in 1981 reported net sales at $363,966,000, an increase of 9.2% over the previous year and earnings at $29,398,000 — a gain of 10.8%.

1982 "New Horizons" _____

The year 1982 was paradoxical for Dr Pepper and as difficult as any in the 98-year history of the Company. It brought new situations that tested its character and resources — expansion and new markets that reached well beyond former horizons. Just as it has done in years past, the management met the problems head-on by changing directions in some important areas.

In January the Company began initial distribution of Dr Pepper in the Netherlands through Bavaria, Ltd., the fourth largest bottler in the area. The new franchisee, headquartered in Lieshout, Holland, implemented the most extensive advertising campaign ever launched on Dr Pepper in an international market.

Bavaria, Ltd., was founded in 1719 as a brewery and is a seventh-generation family-owned business. The advertising slogan used in their Dr Pepper introduction was "The friendly new soft drink with a funny name."

On February 2, 1982 Dr Pepper Company acquired the world-wide Canada Dry business from Norton Simon for a sum of $155 million.

This represented a major step for the Company, both financially and structurally. At the time there were 185 domestic bottlers franchised to distribute Canada Dry products and another 180 licensed to sell in more than 80 foreign countries.

The Canada Dry brands started with "McLaughlin's Pale Dry Ginger Ale" in 1904 and had grown to include Club Soda and Tonic Water and became America's number one line of mixers.

These products, combined with Dr Pepper and Welch's flavors, comprised about 10% of the total industry share of volume with Welch's grape the leader in the flavor segment.

Other acquisitions that marked 1982 as a growth year for the Company included franchise rights and bottling operations of Big Red Bottling Co. of San Antonio, Inc., which were incorporated into the Company's Dr Pepper bottling operations in that market.

Later in the year, on October 29, franchise rights to Dr Pepper, Canada Dry, Seven-Up and a line of flavors were acquired from Roberson Beverages serving a large portion of Eastern North Carolina and on December 8, 1982 franchise rights to Royal Crown soft drinks in San Antonio and Houston became a part of the Company's existing bottling operations in these markets.

The final acquisition in 1982, on December 10, was franchise rights to Dr Pepper for Sherman, Texas which is contiguous to the Company's Dallas-Fort Worth franchise.

To help finance these ambitious acquisitions, the Company, on September 1, sold 2.5 million shares of Dr Pepper common stock in a public offering, reducing its debt by $33.9 million.

Meanwhile, Dr Pepper distribution was expanding further into foreign markets. Another entry was Britvic of England, a division of Allied Beverages, Inc., a large United Kingdom conglomerate handling beer, spirits, wines, soft drinks and food products with annual sales totaling five billion dollars.

Distribution areas for the firm, in addition to the United Kingdom, included Scotland, Wales and the Channel Islands serving a population of approximately 56 million. Headquarters for Britvic are based in Chelmsford.

Initial distribution of Dr Pepper began April 5, with heavy media coverage and extensive sampling and promotion.

Big scale promotions were the order of the year for Dr Pepper in '82, both seasonal and regional. A winter event sponsored by Pennsylvania Dr Pepper bottlers on March 5–6 was the pro-am ski races at Camelback in the Poconos near Tannersville, Pennsylvania, a repeat promotion from 1981. As one of America's top winter sports events, it attracted skiers from Pennsylvania, New Jersey, Delaware, New York and Maryland — and more than one million visitors.

From mid-May through June 30, Dr Pepper conducted its major promotion of the year — a "Millionaire Sweepstakes" which offered a prize of $1,000,000 to the winner. Complete details were presented to bottlers with sweepstakes entry blanks available for distribution in grocery stores across the U.S.

The program attracted more than 98% bottler participation and made marketing history by offering the largest cash prize ever awarded an individual by an American consumer goods company.

Ironically, it failed to produce returns commensurate with the prize which went to Robert A. Healey, a New Jersey resident.

Presenter of the prize was actor Marvin Miller who delivered nearly 200 checks for $1,000,000 each as "Michael Anthony" on the Millionaire TV series.

Following this was a regional promotion on September 25–28 in Wildwood, New Jersey, the International Pro-Am Bike Race sponsored by Dr Pepper. It was the largest bike race in the U.S. attracting riders and enthusiasts from eleven countries including more than 200 professionals. One event was a Dr Pepper Scholarship Race offering amateur riders $20,000 in Series E U.S. Bonds.

Another mid-year Dr Pepper promotion was the Texas Renaissance Festival in Houston, Texas which attracted over a quarter-million visitors. The Dr Pepper Bottling Company of Cleveland, Ohio teamed up with the Cleveland Junior Olympics to sponsor athletic competition for children in that area. In Albuquerque,

New Mexico, the Dr Pepper bottler sponsored a special olympics event involving two thousand people.

At the 55th annual Shenandoah Apple Blossom Festival in Winchester, Virginia, Dr Pepper was represented by sports celebrity Charlie Waters of the Dallas Cowboys in the parade and pageantry. Since 1939 the Dr Pepper Bottling Company of Winchester sponsored a celebrity for the event.

In Dallas, the world's largest soft drink display containing 116,000 cases, over 2 1/2 million bottles and cans valued at over $1,000,000 was built in a large shopping mall. Twenty-five cents from the sale of each case went to the Society for Crippled Children, an Easter Seal affiliate serving the Dallas area.

The year brought significant new product development for all soft drink brands, and Dr Pepper entered the market with its new Pepper Free drink — both caffeine free and sugar free. It was first among the Pepper-type soft drinks to be introduced.

The "Be A Pepper" theme took several new turns in 1982. It included a new song and a revised theme line, placing more emphasis on retrial and taste, as suggested in the tagline . . . "To Be A Pepper, All You Gotta Do Is Taste." And it was also the year that Dr Pepper's Pied Pepper, David Naughton, moved on to the world of movies and television. David had played an instrumental role in establishing "Be A Pepper" as one of the all-time Dr Pepper campaigns, and he would be difficult to replace. But two were found — a young and an old replacement . . . Scott Baio, the teenage idol from the TV series "Happy Days," and that loveable scarecrow from the "Wizard Of Oz," Ray Bolger. Another commercial, where Peppers walked up walls and on ceilings, also walked off with the coveted Clio Award as the best soft drink commercial of the year.

The 1982 Annual Dr Pepper bottler meeting was held in Boston September 26–28 with 1,800 bottlers, plant managers and suppliers taking part in the two-day meeting.

Theme of the program was "Pepper Pride," designed to capture the spirit of bottlers. A return to basics was the underlying message of the Dr Pepper presentations with renewed emphasis on partnership between the Company and its bottlers.

A touch of the American Revolution, Boston Harbor, lobster boil and obviously Dr Pepper combined the old and the new and the best of Boston for a revolutionary experience.

An important and historic announcement at the meeting was the formulation of a "Caffeine Free Dr Pepper." Historic indeed since Dr Pepper was first introduced in 1885 as a "Caffeine Free"

drink. Its founders placed great emphasis on this fact in its advertising based obviously on general misconceptions of the product.

Earlier in the year 7-Up Company had launched a broadscale attack on the safety of caffeine. Dr Pepper Company, along with other major soft drink firms, was being challenged to assure consumers there was no foundation for the charge. An official announcement was issued by the Company stating, "Caffeine is a safe and important component to the flavor of Dr Pepper and Sugar Free Dr Pepper. We are not aware of any scientific evidence that caffeine in Dr Pepper has had a detrimental effect on the health of any person. This belief is substantiated by the most complete study on the safety of caffeine in soft drinks ever submitted to the Federal Drug Administration."

However, the pressure from wide publicity about caffeine led the Company to introduce Pepper Free and Sugar Free Pepper Free in late 1982. Pepper Free was regular Dr Pepper with sweetener, but without caffeine, and Sugar Free Pepper Free was both sugar free and caffeine free, using a combination of aspartame and saccharin as the sweetener. The products did not reach the market until early 1983 and Sugar Free Pepper Free was the first Pepper-type soft drink to use aspartame.

A signal honor came to Dr Pepper Company in the closing months of '82 when its Chairman and CEO, W. W. Clements, was inducted into Beverage World's Hall of Fame. He was one of seventeen so honored over the years for their dedication and leadership in the soft drink industry. Clements was completing his 47th year with Dr Pepper.

The award was made to Clements at the Annual National Soft Drink Association Conference held in Atlanta on November 30,

Dr Pepper was introduced in 1885 as a "Caffeine Free" drink.

which broke all previous attendance records for an NSDA gathering. More than 14,500 were registered for the two-day assembly of member bottlers operating a $20 billion industry. Norman A. Sisisky, president of the Dr Pepper Bottling Company of Petersburg, Va. was retiring president of NSDA.

Capturing Dr Pepper's top per capita honors for 1982 was the Dr Pepper Bottling Company of Elk City, Oklahoma where annual Dr Pepper sales are consistently high.

The mixture of events during 1982, unlike any in the past, brought also a mixture of results. Net earnings were $12,474,000, down 58.3%, and the first downturn for the Company in 24 years; while sales peaked at $516,136,000, up 39% over 1981.

In retrospect, it set the stage for other drastic changes that would follow.

1983 "Special Promotions" _____

First on Dr Pepper's 1983 calendar of events was the traditional New Year's Rockin' Eve Party televised from Times Square in New York with Dick Clark hosting and Barry Manilow as headline entertainer. Following, on New Year's Day, were the two nationally televised parades, The Tournament of Roses in Pasadena where the Dr Pepper float won the "Judges Special Award," and the Cotton Bowl Parade in Dallas with Dr Pepper's entry capturing the "President's Award."

Between the three events, Dr Pepper exposure on opening day of the new year reached an audience of millions both national and international.

The Company's marketing agenda picked up from the previous year to continue special promotions, many now being tailored for individual markets. In Great Britain, Britvic had just concluded a successful promotion tour of the kids from "Fame," a popular American TV series.

The Apple Blossom Festival in Winchester, Virginia, an early springtime event on the Dr Pepper schedule, featured Gary Hogeboom, popular young quarterback for the Dallas Cowboys, as the Dr Pepper celebrity.

In Mason, Texas nearly 400 tennis buffs from Central Texas participated in a tournament sponsored by the local Dr Pepper bottler. In Ottawa, Illinois the Willet family celebrated its 50th anniversary with a Dr Pepper promotion, and in Cleveland, Ohio it was a tie-in for Dr Pepper with a big flower and home show. In Jefferson City, Missouri the bottler sponsored an incentive program offering attractive merchandise prizes; in San Antonio, Texas Dr Pepper participated in "Kissworld," a lifestyle fair sponsored by KISS-FM radio.

Kitchener Beverages, Ltd., in Ontario, Canada marked its 45th anniversary with a series of special events, while the Orangeville Bottling Company, Ltd. in Ontario West observed its 75th anniversary with special retail promotions. Many bottlers used the introduction of Pepper Free Dr Pepper as a promotion vehicle.

During a conference of world leaders in Williamsburg, Virginia, hosted by President Ronald Reagan, Dr Pepper and Canada Dry products were featured on the bill of fare.

The Abilene, Texas bottler exercised his ingenuity by sponsoring a "Cruise Night" with early vintage automobiles competing for awards. The parade route led them to a number of fast food drive-in restaurants that were offering Dr Pepper specials.

Many bottlers adapted promotions to fit their own specific needs. In Monroe, Louisiana it was a sweepstakes display involving nearly 500 dealers that produced a 21% increase in Dr Pepper sales during a twelve-week period. The Dallas, Texas bottler blitzed the market with a vending campaign that placed some 1,200 new Dr Pepper units in the four-week drive.

The Corbin, Kentucky bottler tied his summer promotion to a country-style festival and offered local dealers handsome prizes for special displays. In Lewiston, Idaho the bottler sponsored a Dr Pepper entry in the annual two-day Snake River Boat Race and sampled the 10,000 spectators with Dr Pepper during the event.

Promotions in foreign markets were gaining momentum in 1983. In Holland, Bavaria Ltd. sponsored a Dr Pepper Beetle Club for owners of Volkswagon Beetles who made periodic visits to points of local interest.

Trial and conversion became the key elements in Dr Pepper advertising during '83 and the "Be A Pepper" theme was changed to "Dr Pepper Made A Pepper Out Of Me." This themeline was the payoff to a very single-minded call to action — "Try it, Try it, Try it!"

But it was no longer the days of the Most Misunderstood where the oddball tried to convert the masses . . . it was many Dr Pepper drinkers trying to convert the last holdouts.

Television and radio continued to be the major media vehicles with a TV commercial "Baseball" winning the Bronze Lion award at the famous Cannes Film Festival.

Sugar Free Dr Pepper advertising was centered on convincing people to try the great taste, but it also assured them that it would help them look great. It was a very phonetic campaign from a "Hmmm Hmmm" to a "Wheet Whoo" (Whistle).

An important announcement in September was the Company's authorization of aspartame as a sweetener ingredient in its low calorie soft drinks including Sugar Free Dr Pepper and Sugar Free Canada Dry Ginger Ale. Aspartame's primary attribute was that, like conventional sugar, it leaves no aftertaste. The U.S. Food and Drug Administration had approved aspartame for use in other food products as early as 1981, but had only recently extended its approval to soft drinks.

A new advertising theme for Dr Pepper was announced in the Annual Dr Pepper Bottler Meeting held in Los Angeles October 2-4 — "Hold out for the out-of-the-ordinary — Hold out for Dr Pepper." It would become the basis for the Company's 1984 ad campaign.

In concert with the location of the meeting, presentations of 1984 Dr Pepper advertising took on a Hollywood production format with talented entertainers in dramatic situations. The overall objectives, however, were the same as in previous meetings — to lay before the bottlers complete plans for marketing Dr Pepper in the coming year. Presenters stressed that Dr Pepper's competitive edge was its unique taste and urged bottlers to capitalize on this advantage.

New, larger and more dominant graphics originally adapted for use on vendors and vehicles, were introduced also on Dr Pepper packaging which would begin appearing at the start of 1984. A new advertising theme would also be used for both Dr Pepper and Sugar Free Dr Pepper.

Sampling activity on Dr Pepper was at a new high in '83. In Jackson, Mississippi the bottler developed an ingenious vehicle for his market, a miniature "Ye Olde Tyme Sampler," carrying the 1900 vintage trademark, "Dr Pepper - King of Beverages."

Joyce Beverages in Chicago sponsored a Dr Pepper Swim Meet with 60 teams and 767 swimmers competing. It was a three-day event and the fifth annual meet sponsored by the company.

Dr Pepper had the unusual opportunity to sponsor commemorative cans in connection with the annual football rivalry between the armed services academies. For the 1983 game between Army and Navy and between Army and the Air Force, the company offered specially designed cans of Dr Pepper which helped generate enthusiasm for the two games.

Dr Pepper bottlers in Denver and Colorado Springs utilized TV extensively and salesmen were successful in building nearly 1,200 full-price displays in promoting the Army-Air Force game. Complimentary souvenir cans were presented to all officers from the two academies.

For the Army-Navy game played in the Rose Bowl, Dr Pepper bottlers at several points became involved in the promotion, including Honolulu, Jacksonville, Florida and Norfolk, Virginia.

Sales success from the commemorative cans at both games was enhanced by the prestigious exposure for Dr Pepper among the Armed Services.

Out of the midst of these and other fast-moving marketing activities, as aggresive and far reaching as they were, it became evident to the Company that it was not keeping pace with its major competitors. The race for market share had resolved itself into a discount battle between major brands.

With heavy indebtedness, due to extensive expansion and new acquisitions, Dr Pepper Company was finding it increasingly difficult to compete. Never, in the 98-year history of Dr Pepper, had it not been a viable competitor. It was strictly a matter of increased demands on financial resources.

After many weeks of study, analysis and thorough deliberation, the management elected to seek a partner. Following numerous conferences with qualified financial analysts, Dr Pepper Company and Forstmann Little & Co., a private investment and banking firm of New York, agreed to a tentative merger whereby Forstmann Little would acquire Dr Pepper at a price of $22 per share. At the time, Dr Pepper stock was listed on the NYSE at $17 5/8 per share.

An agreement in principle was approved by the Company's board of directors on December 4. Forstmann Little was prepared to invest $150 million of capital in the transaction and had received letters of commitment from a group of banks for the balance of the purchase price.

Consummation of the transaction was subject to execution of the definitive merger agreement, approval by Dr Pepper stockholders, execution and closing of definitive bank loan agreements and fulfillment of other customary conditions.

As of November 16, 1983 there were 23,297,153 shares of Dr Pepper common stock outstanding and 409,192 shares issuable upon the exercise of outstanding employee options.

Forstmann Little & Co. was a private investment firm specializing in leveraged buyouts. Dr Pepper Company was the third largest soft drink manufacturer marketing its products under the private label brands of Dr Pepper, Canada Dry and Welch's carbonated soft drinks.

The transaction was on schedule until December 6, when the Company received a letter on behalf of Castle & Cooke, Inc., and other investors, proposing to acquire Dr Pepper Company through a cash merger for a total purchase price of $560 million.

Specifics of the Castle & Cooke offer contemplated $550 million in bank financing to be secured by Dr Pepper assets, $125 million subordinated debt, and $50 million equity.

Dr Pepper Company agreed that it and Lazard Freres & Co., its financial advisers, would study the proposal which would expire on December 12, 1983.

Meanwhile, on December 9, Forstmann Little & Co., advised the Company it had entered into a definitive loan agreement with a group of banks for the amount of financing necessary to affect the acquisition of Dr Pepper Company for a total consideration of $624 million, including assumption of $110 million of existing debt.

On December 10, the Company announced that a committee of its outside directors had carefully considered both proposals and it was their opinion that the best interest of the stockholders of the Company was to proceed with the Forstmann Little offer.

Basis for the decision was that the proposal by Castle & Cooke was highly conditional in nature and could not be defined as a firm offer.

The action led to litigation on the part of Castle & Cooke which later was dropped, as was their offer. The year thus ended with the final merger pending the vote of stockholders which would be held at the annual meeting in Dallas on February 28, 1984.

A fitting climax to 1983 was the timely recognition given to two soft drink industry giants, both major figures in the Dr Pepper bottler organization. Ed O'Reilly, president of the New York Dr Pepper franchise, and John W. "Bill" Davis, veteran Dr Pepper bottler in Roanoke, Virginia.

O'Reilly was named Beverage Industry "Man of the Year" by editors of Beverage Industry Magazine, and Davis was inducted into the "Beverage World Hall of Fame."

Both received the honors at the National Soft Drink Association annual meeting held in Houston, Texas December 5–7.

O'Reilly was a 23-year industry veteran; Davis, with 48 years, pioneered Dr Pepper distribution in Virginia and built the Roanoke franchise into the highest Dr Pepper per capita market in the country. He served as a member of the Dr Pepper Company board of directors for 20 years, retiring in 1975, and was a member of the NSDA executive board 19 years.

Dr Pepper's origin and history were reaffirmed in 1983 when Waco, Texas, its birthplace, for the 17th time became the top Dr Pepper per capita market in the U.S.

Total net sales for Dr Pepper Company for the year amounted to $560,415,000, for an increase of 8.6% over 1982, with earnings at $21,590,000, an increase of 73%.

1984 "An Out-Of-The Ordinary Year" _____

The corporate history of Dr Pepper will point to 1984 as a transient year for the Company. Change of direction was eminent as new circumstances confronted the Company that would have great impact on its future.

In spite of its phenomenal success, which began in the thirties and accelerated rapidly in the sixties and seventies, it had reached a plateau which called for comprehensive analysis. Company strategy over the past 20 years had been sound. Innovative advertising and marketing brought industry recognition to Dr Pepper and its distinctive taste enabled it to climb to the No. 3 market share position among soft drink brands.

History painfully reveals, however, that success does not automatically repeat itself. One company president frequently reminded his associates, " We don't have to be the biggest to be the best," and Dr Pepper over the years has been out front in many categories; an innovator, originator and leader.

It was wisely understood that in order for Dr Pepper to continue its forward progress, some new direction would be in order. Thus the move to reduce the Company's indebtedness, consolidate its gains and find new operating capital became the number one priority as 1984 got under way. This action was seen by Company management as a positive way to deal with Dr Pepper's present and future.

The year began, however, with the long-standing traditional events. Dick Clark, for the 12th successive year, hosted Dr Pepper's nationally televised New Year's Rock'n Eve Party from

Principals in the leverage buyout of Dr Pepper Company (left to right), Nicholas C. Forstmann, Theodore J. Forstmann and Wm. Brian Little, general partners in a privately held New York investment firm.

Times Square with Barry Manilow sparking the entertainment.

Dr Pepper sponsored floats in the Annual Tournament of Roses Parade in Pasadena and the Cotton Bowl Parade in Dallas were again viewed by millions on the scene and over live TV; and again, as they have done repeatedly in the past, Dr Pepper float entries won special awards. In Pasadena it was the "Humor Trophy" and in Dallas the "Mayor's Award."

The major and historic event on Dr Pepper's early 1984 calendar was the special meeting of Company stockholders at the Fairmont Hotel in Dallas on February 28. Purpose of the meeting was to canvas the votes of stockholders on a proposed merger with Forstmann Little & Co., in a leveraged buyout of Dr Pepper Company.

Principals in the transaction were Nicholas C. Forstmann, Theodore J. Forstmann and Wm. Brian Little, general partners in a privately-held New York investment firm.

Result of the meeting was an overwhelming 16.7 million of Dr Pepper Company's shares, or 71.7 percent, voting in favor of the Forstmann Little offer. The affirmative vote represented 93.35 percent of the total 17.5 million shares voted, thus consummating the deal.

A total of 652,596 shares, or 2.8 percent, voted against the merger and approximately 162,880 shares abstained. Total shares eligible to vote amounted to 23,296,217, held by 22,000 registered shareowners. A two-thirds affirmative vote was necessary to approve the merger, thus making Dr Pepper a privately-owned company.

Stockholders received $22 for each share of common stock totaling $647 million in the transaction. It was announced that approximately fifteen officers and employees of Dr Pepper Company would acquire an equity interest in the new company. Clements was named chairman and a director in the new corporation, along with the three general partners of Forstmann Little & Co.

Such a major change from previous operations could not escape some emotional misgivings on the part of the management. At a formal dinner held in the banquet room of the Dallas Museum of Art on February 28, all directors of the Company were signally honored for their valuable services.

Formal dinner honoring members of the Dr Pepper Company board of directors for their valuable service, seated (left to right) Edwin L. Cox, A. F. Sloan, W. R. Roberson, Jr., Lamar Hunt and Mrs. Rita C. Clements. Back row (left to right) Pat W. McNamara, Jr., Richard A. Zimmerman, W. W. Clements, Richard Q. Armstrong and John P. Thompson.

In expressing appreciation to the group, W. W. Clements, chairman, was optimistic that Dr Pepper would continue its long record of progress. To underscore his remarks and add a note of levity, he concluded with "It's not over 'til the fat lady sings," whereupon Melody Jones, talented actress and operatic singer, demonstrated his remarks with a dramatic aria.

To fully appraise bottlers of the newly-formed Company, a series of five regional meetings were held in Dallas, Atlanta, New York, Chicago and San Francisco.

In company with the change in ownership were others in the area of Dr Pepper advertising for 1984, two in particular relating to previous campaigns. First, it signaled a return to the original, unorthodox and even outrageous advertising that had proved to be successful in the early and mid-seventies.

"The Most Misunderstood" and "Most Original" campaigns had won attention for Dr Pepper among consumers because they were based on essential truth, the original and unquestionably different taste of Dr Pepper. The "Be A Pepper" campaign in prior years had drifted into the mainstream of soft drink advertising and, while it served Dr Pepper well, it was time to return to the true personality of the brand.

The second notable change was recognition that the Dr Pepper taste was the same whether it was Dr Pepper, Sugar Free Dr Pepper or Pepper-Free. Thus a single unified strategy was adopted for all Dr Pepper brands that extolled its great asset, its unique and original taste.

Dr Pepper's 1984 radio-TV campaign introduced a new set of personalities, some historic in nature who reject the usual and hold out for the unique. The tagline, "Hold out for the out-of-the-ordinary" suggested that consumers "Hold out for Dr Pepper!"

With the soft drink market deluged by new products, Dr Pepper suggested to consumers "Hold out for the out of the ordinary." After 100 years there was still nothing that tasted like Dr Pepper on the scene.

Television commercials were going left when you thought they were going right; one featuring the famous hunchback who finally conveys that he only wants a Dr Pepper. This 60-second commercial captured the attention of viewers-consumers and won a Clio Award for "the best non-alcoholic beverage commercial," and a

new drive periods would be conducted and tied in with an "Out-of-The-Ordinary" sweepstakes promotion.

An important announcement at the meeting was a change in name for Sugar-Free Dr Pepper to Diet Dr Pepper. Reason for the change was to more accurately identify the product with competitive brands for the benefit of consumers.

It was also announced that some of the popular 1985 advertising features would be updated and repeated in 1986 including "Space Cowboy" and "Godzilla Two."

A major subject on the Las Vegas program was the 1986 promotion of the Dr Pepper Fountain-Foodservice Division. Based on 1985 experience, bottlers had been highly successful in this area. National account sales from the division for the year were up nearly 40%.

A convention in Las Vegas would have to include the atmosphere and glamour that encompass the city. Caesar's Palace, the Dr Pepper convention hotel, offered a galaxy of attractions and luxury accommodations for the bottler guests.

On opening night of the meeting bottlers were informally entertained at a "Blockbuster's Party" on Fremont Street in downtown Las Vegas. The following night they enjoyed an "Evening Under the Stars" on McDermott Plaza at the University of Las Vegas. Following a gourmet dinner was a stage presentation headlined by Linda Ronstadt and a cast of 200 from Up With People.

On Tuesday morning, October 1, in the Sports Pavilion of Caesar's Palace was a brunch meeting billed as "A Toast to the Second Century."

Following a summary of the two-day program and a challenge to enter the second century of Dr Pepper, bottler achievers for the year were given a festive farewell on their voyage to South America by the Smothers Brothers.

The top per capita award for Dr Pepper in its centennial year went to the bottler franchise in Dodge City, Kansas, where sales have run consistently high. In 1984 the Dodge City market ranked third in national per capita standings.

With the close of business for 1985, Dr Pepper rings down the curtain on its "100 Original Years." One of the major accomplishments of the Company during the year was its reduction of outstanding indebtedness from $640 million to approximately $170 million, bringing finances into a very manageable position. While this was being done the marketing investment was substantially increased to provide strong sales support for Dr Pepper in 1986.

Recorded here are only highlights of the Company's activities during the period 1980–1985, the first 95 years having been documented in "Dr Pepper - King of Beverages," published in 1980.

For the record we have made available for those in the future many of the important events which have shaped Dr Pepper's past. The value from this information will be determined by those who will use it in shaping Dr Pepper's future. From it all, beginning with its origin in 1885, Dr Pepper is recognized as no ordinary product.

Based on all the evidence, Dr Pepper's message of the future does indeed become . . . "Hold out for out-of-the-ordinary - hold out for Dr Pepper!"

The complete story of the origin of Dr Pepper, the founding of the company and its early beginning was published in an earlier volume titled "Dr Pepper - King of Beverages." For the benefit of readers of this edition, however, we present here a brief version of that narration.

ALDERTON THE ORIGINATOR

Charles Courtice Alderton, a young Englishman, inherited the incentive that led his fellow countrymen to discover the secrets of liquid carbonation. His parents had migrated from England to Brooklyn, New York where Alderton was born on June 21, 1857.

To receive his preliminary formal education, Alderton went to England where he attended a college in Stowmarket, after which he returned to Brooklyn just as John Soule and Horace Greeley were spreading the word, "Go west, young man, go west." Go west young Alderton did to attend medical school at the University of Texas in Galveston, Texas.

Graduating with an M.D., Alderton elected to work as a pharmacist, moving to Waco, Texas to join W. B. Morrison in his Old Corner Drug Store. And here is where it all began and where Alderton would experiment with some of his knowledge of effervescent waters.

He observed that patrons of the Old Corner Drug soda fountain soon tired of the standard fountain flavors. He confirmed this by his own taste experiments which led him to concoct a series of mixtures to find a more palatable drink.

After a variety of combinations of fruit extracts from the fountain, he finally hit upon one that was particularly pleasing to his taste. Carefully measuring the different flavors and after numerous samplings on his own, he invited Morrison to try his new drink.

As Morrison took his first sip, eyebrows went up expressing his surprise and pleasure. From that point, Alderton and Morrison tested their own acceptance of the new drink repeatedly and were satisfied they had an original.

Next came the big test; would their fountain patrons like it? The only way they would find out was to suggest they try it. Try it they did and the reaction was even more exciting. Alderton's drink caught on fast and soon customers were asking for "Doc Alderton's drink." It was very much an "original" then and still is, after 100 years, raising eyebrows of those who enjoy their first taste of Dr Pepper.

Alderton the originator, Morrison the promoter, Lazenby the founder, left to right, are the principals in the origin of Dr Pepper. Each played his respective role in the launching of a great American enterprise.

MORRISON THE PROMOTER _____

If Charles Alderton played his role as inventor of Dr Pepper well, so did Wade Morrison, proprietor of the Old Corner Drug in Waco, Texas where it all took place. Morrison, likewise a pharmacist, was first to recognize the uniqueness of Dr Pepper and its promising potential. He played a major role by encouraging Alderton and helping him with the experiments.

It was Morrison, also, who became the promoter of Alderton's drink suggesting that fountain patrons try it. He well could have coined the phrase, "Try it, you'll like it," which some 80 years later turned up as a national ad campaign slogan for Dr Pepper.

Morrison, like Alderton, had earlier heeded Greeley's advice, moving west from Rural Retreat, Virginia, where he worked in a drug store owned by Dr. Charles Pepper. The doctor had an attractive teenage daughter who caught young Morrison's eye and soon a budding romance developed. The doctor, however, thought the romance was premature and discouraged the affair.

Morrison moved to Waco, Texas to work in a drug store owned by John W. Castles. It wasn't long before he became a partner with Castles and the store became known as Castles & Morrison Drugs.

A year later Morrison purchased the store from Castles and changed its name to Morrison's Old Corner Drug.

He had not forgotten his earlier infatuation with the Virginia doctor's daughter and spoke often about it to his friends. At this point, someone brought up the question of the name of Alderton's new drink now being served regularly at Morrison's Drug Store fountain.

One thing led to another and finally it was suggested they name the drink after the Virginia doctor, the idea being that it might curry favor for Morrison.

Out of this unique situation, Dr Pepper acquired its name, stemming from Morrison's youthful romance with the daughter of the Virginia doctor.

Conjecture, or perhaps romanticism, had Morrison returning to Rural Retreat, Virginia where he supposedly married the doctor's daughter which was only fantasy. Carrie Jeffress, a young lady he met while working in Round Rock, Texas, became his bride.

LAZENBY THE FOUNDER _____

Dr Pepper had been been invented at the soda fountain, it had met with great favor among those who had tasted it and was gaining in popularity in and around Waco, Texas.

Its inventor, Charles C. Alderton, a pharmacist working at Morrison's Old Corner Drug, had no designs on developing the drink. It had fortuitously been named after a doctor in Rural Retreat, Virginia.

Morrison, proprietor of the Old Corner Drug, and Alderton, the originator of Dr Pepper, soon ran into a problem. Orders for the new drink from other drug store fountains had reached a point where they were having difficulty producing the syrup in their store.

Customers were waiting outside for Morrison's Drug to open, unaware that Dr Pepper history was about to be made inside — and Charles Alderton would ask . . . "Would you like to try something different?"

Robert S. Lazenby, a patron of the store, had tasted the new Dr Pepper drink repeatedly and liked it. His was a valuable endorsement, being a beverage chemist of note and owner of the Circle "A" Ginger Ale Bottling Company in Waco, which he had started in 1884.

It was more than chance that brought Morrison to Lazenby's office to discuss his producing the Dr Pepper flavoring syrup in his bottling plant.

Lazenby was already favorably impressed with Dr Pepper and it took no great amount of persuasion from Morrison to get him interested.

Lazenby, however, being the beverage expert, insisted on doing further research on the drink and ended up making a number of refinements in its quality and flavor.

This alliance between Morrison and Lazenby grew as did the sales and distribution of Dr Pepper. Lazenby soon recognized further potential from bottling the drink and, in partnership with Morrison, formed a new company, The Artesian Mfg. & Bottling Works.

They introduced the drink first in Hiram Codd's internal ball-stoppered bottle which had been on the market some twelve years. A new trademark was developed advertising "Dr Pepper Phos-Ferrates" as unique and different from any other carbonated drink. Wording on the label stated "Good at fountains and in bottles."

Indeed it was and it rapidly gained in popularity, not only in and around Waco but throughout Central Texas.

Robert S. Lazenby went on to become the sole owner of the company which later became The Dr Pepper Company.

The first Dr Pepper bottle was a classic enclosure, using a fiber ring in the neck and a floating marble as a stopper. These are rare because small boys broke the bottle after drinking the Dr Pepper to get the marble.

The first Dr Pepper glass tumbler would today win an art award for "Simplicity" - that is if there were still one around. It would also bring a handsome price as a "collectible."

The Liquid Sunshine idea attracted such favorable consumer attention that R. S. Lazenby decided to identify Dr Pepper under the same label. Bottle labels on Dr Pepper in limited markets featured the sunburst art and some trademarks included the title.

Lazenby's Liquid Sunshine was sold both at fountains and in bottles. Made from grapefruit juice, invert sugar with no preservatives or color added, it was reportedly the first grapefruit drink on the market.

LAZENBY'S LIQUID SUNSHINE

In the course of early Dr Pepper history there are indications that the drink could well have become known and advertised as "Liquid Sunshine;" and who can say that it was inappropriate or that it would not have been a good name for the drink?

R. S. Lazenby, perfecter of the Dr Pepper formula and founder of the Dr Pepper Company, was a man of great originality. The wide assortment of promotional items he introduced and his imaginative ideas for advertising Dr Pepper are evidence of his ingenuity.

His reputation as a beverage chemist had attracted wide attention which led to his being commissioned by the U. S. Government to conduct a five-year experiment in the Texas Rio Grande Valley to discover a way to preserve important vitamins from grapefruit through a canning process. His experiments proved successful and resulted in some of the first packaging of grapefruit juice.

From his experiments Lazenby introduced a new bottled soft drink made from grapefruit which he called Liquid Sunshine. He registered the trademark and formed The Liquid Sunshine Company which was located at 4515 Fannin Street in Houston, Texas. Records show that he operated bottling plants in Austin and Waco, Texas as The Liquid Sunshine Bottling Co.

It appears that Lazenby had contemplated also including Dr Pepper under the Sunshine label. In St. Louis, where he had introduced Dr Pepper as early as 1904, he produced a trademark for his Dr Pepper bottle label which featured the sunburst design. Some Dr Pepper trademarks also appeared using the title. Dr Pepper was being bottled in St. Louis by the Mineral Water Works while a second bottling company, Carse & Ohlweiler in Rock Island, Illinois, was also using the same label.

There is no record of explanation of Lazenby's plans for the use of the Liquid Sunshine label but indications are that he seriously considered it for promoting Dr Pepper even though he had originated it for his grapefruit drink.

Some of the advertising produced by Lazenby graphically describes Dr Pepper as "Liquid Sunshine." One newspaper ad, appearing in the Bremond, Texas Enterprise in 1913, gave a colorful and imaginative explanation of Dr Pepper as "Solar energy-liquid sunshine." (See reprint)

Dr. Pepper
KING OF BEVERAGES

LIQUID SUNSHINE

Scientists tell us that all space is an ocean of ether in which our solar system swims, and that all life, animal and vegetable, is derived from the sun's energy, transmitted to our planet by this ether. Plant life organizes this energy for us in natures laboratory. As animals we then partake of natures bountiful store and the sun's energy. Certain fruits, nuts and sugar cane represent this energy and vitality best. We have found this great natural law, and we combine these substances with distilled water. The name we give our combination is Dr. Pepper.

Dr. Pepper is liquid sunlight. As the sun rules and governs the day, so should you govern your appetite. Eat and drink to build up the cells that are broken down by fatigue, mental or physical. Drink a beverage that promotes cell building, not one that simply deadens the sensory nerves. Drink Dr. Pepper. Solar energy-liquid sunshine. Vim, vigor, vitality—that is what Dr. Pepper means. Try it. On sale at all fountains and in bottles. It's made in Texas. It's profits are spent in Texas to promote Texas industries,

DR. PEPPER CO. Waco, Texas

Lazenby wanted consumers to have good reason for drinking Dr Pepper as expressed in this advertisement appearing in the Bremond, Texas Enterprise newspaper on June 20, 1913. Drinking "solar energy-liquid sunshine" sounds like reason enough.

DR PEPPER ADVERTISING

. . . Object d' Art!

Art is a window through which we view the past.
It portrays people, places and products that
have not been erased by time.

One of the great mediums in American history is advertising. It has left its indelible mark on every facet of each generation; it has influenced masses of people and brought major change in the lives of individuals; it has achieved a status of "Object d' Art" in America.

As early as 1900 Dr Pepper advertising art was recognized and admired for its aesthetic quality. The initial work done was for poster art but it also appeared on many smaller pieces as well, including blotters, book markers, fans, postcards and calendars.

One artist who was particularly prolific at the time was Philip Boileau, a French Canadian born in Quebec in 1864 of a French father and American mother. The father, Baron Charles Boileau, was the French Consul General of Quebec and his wife was Susan Taylor Benton, daughter of well known U.S. Senator Thomas Hart Benton of Missouri.

The Senator was an influential figure in American history with a fascinating career which included a 19th Century street brawl in Memphis with another famous American, Andrew Jackson.

Susan's sister married John C. Freemont who earned fame as an explorer and for his unsuccessful tries at the U.S. Presidency.

Boileau, the artist, spent his early life in England. From there he went to Italy for art training in the specialty which intrigued him, portraits of women.

He claimed American citizenship through his mother and at age 39, while living in New York, was married to Emily Gilbert in 1903. Up until then his work had been unimpressive, but his marriage to Emily changed all that. She became his inspiration, his model and her nickname "Peggy" became his trademark. He did her portrait the year they were married, titling it "Peggy" and suddenly found himself catapulted to fame.

From then on all of his portraits, prints and illustrations were known as "Peggy Heads" after his first success. Boileau was one

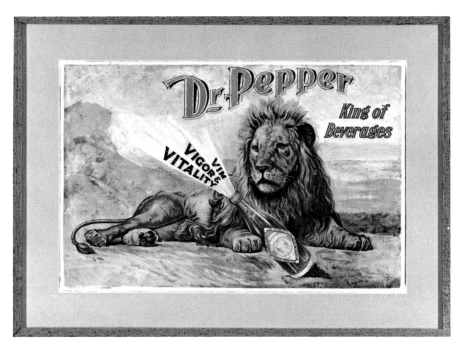

LOUIS STERNKORB
The first major Dr Pepper art piece appeared in 1907 as a painted wall sign in downtown Waco, Texas, where the drink originated. It was done by Louis Sternkorb, local advertising artist, who was hired to do the painting by the Artesian Manufacturing & Bottling Co., bottler of Dr Pepper. The lion figure had been adopted by the company for its official trademark symbol. It was copyrighted in 1907 and used extensively to advertise and promote Dr Pepper some twenty years under the banner "Dr Pepper - King of Beverages."

PHILIP BOILEAU
   Although unsigned, this beautiful Dr Pepper poster girl is thought to be one by Philip Boileau, French Canadian artist of early 1900. Boileau painted many pretty girl posters titling them all "Peggy Heads" in honor of his wife who was his first successful model and whose nickname was Peggy.

of the forerunners to the vast number of artists who have captured feminine beauty and made it the number one object d' art in America.

Although unsigned, the attractive girl on the Dr Pepper poster painted in early 1900 is considered the work of Philip Boileau. Retrieved from a heap of discarded advertising poster art some years ago to become a rare collector's item, it is valued today at $2,000.

Other attractive Dr Pepper art pieces appeared during the period which today are prized by collectors.

It wasn't until the early twenties that contemporary artists began to capture a new style of Dr Pepper art which focuses on the nostalgic settings in rural America. For years large painted Dr Pepper advertising signs dotted the landscape, often in out-of-the-way settings far from the point-of-sale. Other notable products such as Dutch Boy Cleanser, Bull Durham Tobacco, Fletcher's Castoria and Arm & Hammer Baking Soda were also among the rural masterpieces.

They were all done by artists who used barns and other farm buildings as the canvas for their work.

As time passed, farms became abandoned but the buildings and signs remained as graphic reminders of early-day products. Age and deterioration only added to the picturesque settings making them even more conspicuous.

Dr Pepper's age, as it celebrates "100 Original Years," is indelibly etched on the landscape of urban and rural America by these artistic reminders of a soft drink that capitalized on its time.

Through courtesy of a number of prominent contemporary artists, whose sensitive eyes caught a glimpse of the past, we are pleased to present some of their work. It captures the imagination of some; brings back fond memories for others. The original paintings have appeared in numerous gallery exhibits and limited edition prints are highly prized as "collectibles."

Dr Pepper is honored to have become an "Object d' Art" for many outstanding artists beginning with Philip Boileau back in 1900 and for those who today through their imaginative skills, are preserving the heritage of American products.

BERNIE FUCHS
In celebration of its 100th anniversary, the Dr Pepper Company commissioned an original art work by noted illustrator Bernie Fuchs. A limited edition of signed and numbered prints, it is appropriately titled "Sunday Sipping Treat."
Fuch's paintings have appeared in nearly every major national magazine; his illustrations have been featured in a dozen limited edition books for the Franklin Library, along with more than 60 "Profiles" drawings for The New Yorker Magazine. He was commissioned to do portraits of both President Kennedy and President Johnson as part of a U. S. Graphics Exhibition in Russia. He has received every award bestowed by the New York Society of Illustrators and in 1962 was named artist of the year by the Artists Guild of New York. Fuchs was born in O'Fallon, Illinois and graduated from Washington University School of Fine Arts in St. Louis, Missouri. His career began as an illustrator in Detroit, Michigan and he now works and lives in Westport, Connecticut.

HAL WARNICK
   Texas artist Hal Warnick is a Texas Aggie who studied under a dozen of the country's best artists and teachers. Warnick titled his painting "Hill Country Shadows," reflecting the sun's rays on the old Texas & Brazos Valley RR station located in Central Texas. The 1940 vintage Dr Pepper sign on the building caught the shadows but not enough to dim its image for those who still remember the sights and sounds of the trains. Warnick, a full-time artist for some 25 years, operates his own gallery in Dallas. His painting was acquired by Dr Pepper and is now included in the Company's archives.

MICHAEL GARMAN

A most unusual and impressive art piece with Dr Pepper a dominant feature is Michael Garman's three dimensional production titled "Court & Darby Street," a magical twenty-foot-long city street corner that spans time from post-depression to present day. Garman is a master craftsman in three-dimensional sculpture. His "Garman Originals," prized by collectors, are displayed throughout the world and frequently given as a piece of Americana to dignitaries and heads of state. A native Texan, Garman did his apprenticeship in Los Angeles, then spent two years in Central and South America as a photojournalist. He now resides in Colorado Springs, Colorado.

JIM HARRISON

Jim Harrison is one of the country's foremost pictorial artists, specializing in rural scapes that are fast disappearing. He was born in Georgia but his family moved to the tiny crossroads community of Denmark, S.C. As a teenager he worked with an elderly sign painter, J. J. Cornforth, traveling between small towns painting billboards on general stores and barns. Harrison attended the University of South Carolina, majoring in education and fine art. He was good in athletics and considered a coaching career, but his love for art was greater. Despite a rocky beginning with sidewalk art shows from greenwich Village to Palm Springs, the Harrison style soon caught on. In 1977 his one-man show at New York's Hammer Galleries established him as a serious artist and he returned there in 1979 for another successful show. His Dr Pepper barn door bottle sign was one of his popular limited edition prints.

GEORGE BOUTWELL

An accomplished Texas illustrator and artist, George Boutwell of Austin, Texas, was commissioned by the Dr Pepper Company in 1976 to do a series of paintings featuring Dr Pepper in rural settings. Pictured are two of his works illustrating 1950 and 1960 Dr Pepper trademarks. Setting for the 1950 bull's eye sign and rooster was near Luckenbach, Texas, a small Hill Country hamlet, population three, owned by the late Texas folk hero Hondo Crouch. The town became famous as the site of the annual Luckenbach World's Fair and as the title of a popular song recording by Waylon Jennings and Willie Nelson. Boutwell's barn painting of a resident rooster and Dr Pepper adds further distinction to Luckenbach, Texas.

Dr Pepper was originally concocted from a combination of fruit and other natural extracts and its formula has remained basically the same ever since. R. S. Lazenby, founder of the Dr Pepper Company, advertised Dr Pepper as "The pure fruit juice drink." Its unusual and distinctive fruity flavor has made Dr Pepper out-of-the-ordinary during its 100 original years.

* The Exposition was organized May 2, 1902 with David R. Francis as president. Legislative authority was granted for raising the capital of $25,000,000, of which the U.S. Government contributed one-fifth.

The site chosen was within the city limits of St. Louis, including 1,200 acres of Forest Park, long since regarded as one of the great municipal parks in America.

In the exhibit grounds were about 2,500 groups and 1,000 figures in sculptures. Admissions totaled 19,694,855, of which $12,804,616 were paid. Total expenses amounted to $31,586,331; total receipts were $11,952,254.

It was in this setting that Dr Pepper made its first major promotional venture and became one of the popular refreshments and much talked about new carbonated soft drink from Texas. Its taste was entirely new and different, described as "delightful, refreshing, healthful and invigorating."

Dr Pepper was virtually unknown outside of Central Texas where it was first introduced in 1885. It was being bottled and sold by the Circle "A" Ginger Ale Co., in Waco, Texas, a small bottling operation owned and managed by Robert S. Lazenby. He had founded the business in 1883 and was recognized in the area as a skilled beverage chemist.

His Circle "A" brand ginger ale was of extraordinary quality and flavor and soon became outstanding among the leading brands. Lazenby had done extensive research in developing the drink in which he used pure ginger imported from Jamaica.

Further distinction came to the drink when it was the choice beverage served on dining and club cars on crack U.S. passenger trains.

It was this success from Lazenby's Circle "A" Ginger Ale that paved the way for his introduction of Dr Pepper at the St. Louis World's Fair.

First he established a new bottling facility and general operating office in St. Louis under the name Circle "A" Corporation of America. The business was located at 21st and Walnut Streets in a two-story building with basement.

R. S. Lazenby, founder of the Dr Pepper Company, established his Circle "A" Corporation in this building at 21st and Walnut Streets in St. Louis where he bottled Dr Pepper for sale at the 1904 World's Fair and Exposition.

This silver watch fob and band was presented to select guests attending the 1904 St. Louis World's Fair. Engraved on one side of the fob was the official emblem of the Fair; on the reverse side was "The Home of Dr Pepper" in Waco, Texas.

To head up the operation he placed his son-in-law J. B. O'Hara in charge as general manager. Together Lazenby and O'Hara set out to introduce their new drink Dr Pepper at the big world's fair and exposition.

This being Dr Pepper's first major exposure outside of Central Texas, O'Hara, the marketing innovator, wanted to capture the attention of fair-goers for the new drink. Since the Dr Pepper flavor was completely different from any other carbonated drink, he decided to provide guests with some form of popular gift that would draw attention to Dr Pepper.

Every male visitor carried a pocket watch. What better premium than an attractive watch fob souvenir of the fair? To make it authentic the fob was a molded brass and silver overlay replica of the official Exposition medal of honor which was cast in silver. On one side of the official medal was a beautiful figured design and engraved inscription "Silver Medal, Louisiana Purchase Exposition." On the reverse side was inscribed "Universal Exposition, St. Louis, Mo." It was 2″ × 3″ in size.

On the front side of the Dr Pepper watch fob was a cast reproduction of the celebration medal. On its reverse side was a cast illustration of "The Home of Dr Pepper, Waco, Texas." Two sizes of the fob were produced, one 1″ × 1¼″ and another 1¼″ × 2″, each from brass with silver overlay.

For top dignitaries and VIP, however, O'Hara and Lazenby produced a limited number of fobs in silver and, in place of a leather strap, used a beautiful silver link strap engraved with four St. Louis landmark structures. They were St. Louis' famous Union Station, one of the largest and most unique railroad passenger facilities in the United States. Completely under roof, the station could accommodate 32 passenger trains on parallel tracks simultaneously. It also contained a variety of shops, a hotel and movie theater.

Another illustration on the silver strap was of St. Louis' famous Eads Bridge spanning the Mississippi River. It, likewise, was a remarkable structure with double deck to accommodate both railroad and automobile traffic.

These four historic St. Louis landmarks were engraved on a silver watch fob band distributed at the St. Louis fair by Dr Pepper. They are, left to right, the Palace of Machinery, Cascade Gardens, Eads Bridge and Union Station railroad terminal.

A third illustration was the Cascade Gardens featuring a beautiful waterfall in a floral setting that fascinated the thousands of daily Exposition visitors and perhaps set the theme for the many other beauitiful gardens which cover the St. Louis landscape today.

The fourth engraving on the silver Dr Pepper fob strap was the Palace of Machinery, one of the major buildings erected for the Exposition which housed a mammoth exhibit of the latest in manufacturing machinery.

The Dr Pepper fob was one of the prized souvenirs of the St. Louis exposition. Today it is regarded a rare "collectible" and carries a handsome price tag in the antique market.

We discover later, however, a second watch fob premium that Lazenby used in promoting Dr Pepper; a good luck charm that would turn away misfortune and make good things happen. Some called it "Lazenby's Luck Piece," which featured a grinning Billiken. On one side of the fob was the engraved image of the Billiken with the inscription "Grin and begin to win by drinking Dr Pepper." On the reverse side of the fob was an engraving of "The Home of Dr Pepper - Waco, Texas."

An old saying about the Billiken, a universal symbol of good fortune, was "Rub his tummy or tickle his toes, you'll have good luck as the story goes."

Interestingly, both of Lazenby's watch fobs apparently originated in St. Louis. The Billiken was copyrighted soon after the St. Louis World's Fair which leads to believe Lazenby was one of the first to use it in this manner. Further interesting is the role the Billiken has continued to play in St. Louis where, in 1911, it became the nickname of the St. Louis University football players. Although the record of success of the SLU team over the years provides no solid evidence of the luck of the Billiken, it still symbolizes things as they ought to be.

This would be reason enough for Lazenby to place the Billiken on a watch fob to suggest to its owner . . . "Grin and begin to win by drinking Dr Pepper."

For dealers serving Dr Pepper at the St. Louis exposition, Lazenby and O'Hara provided an attractive ceramic syrup urn that drew further attention to the product. As unique as its flavor was its trademark featuring the "Dr Pepper's Phos Ferrates" logo.

A second Dr Pepper watch fob produced soon after the St. Louis fair featured a Billiken, universal symbol of good fortune. The Billiken was adopted in 1911 as a nickname for the St. Louis University football players.

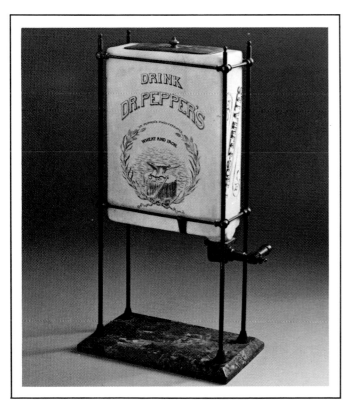

Ceramic syrup urns were a popular new device for dispensing Dr Pepper at the St. Louis World's Fair. The "Phos Ferrates" logo was as unique and different as the Dr Pepper flavor which won favor with many of the fair-goers.

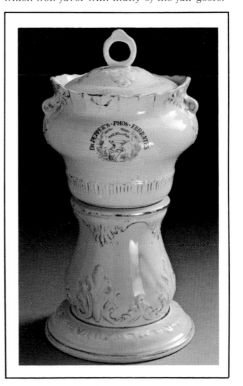

*Athens, Texas cafe owner Fletcher Davis
(1864-1944) innovated and introduced
the first hamburger sandwich at the St. Louis fair.
This photo of Davis was his official
identification as an exhibitor at the fair.*

* Noteworthy it is that Dr Pepper was not the only product originating in Texas to be introduced at the St. Louis fair. In Athens, Texas a young man named Fletcher Davis had opened a small sandwich shop where he "invented" a new specialty to attract customers. It was a ground beef patty between two slices of bread, garnished with mustard, a slice of Bermuda onion and sliced cucumber pickles.

Fletch's sandwich became a big hit with his patrons, so much so that he decided to try it out at the St. Louis World's Fair where he started serving it on a bun and where it got the name "Hamburger."

The story goes that it got this name from Hamburg, Germany where ground beef had been commonly prepared and served in the past. And since there were many Germans living in St. Louis, presumably one of them dubbed it "Hamburger" in honor of their native city.

Regardless, Fletcher Davis of Athens, Texas is credited as the first to prepare and serve it in sandwich form and patrons of the World's Fair in St. Louis were first to enjoy it outside of Athens, Texas. Davis also served fried potatoes with his hamburger which he had learned about from a friend who lived in Paris, Texas. A reporter for the New York Tribune, writing about new foods being served at the Fair, said in his story that Davis was serving "French fried potatoes" with his hamburger, thinking that his friend was from Paris, France.

So it is, two great food items in America, hamburger and french fries, were introduced at the 1904 World's Fair in St. Louis, each with names of foreign extraction.

And what a concurrence also that hamburgers, french fries and Dr Pepper, all "Native Texans" having made their debut in St. Louis in 1904, are still companion foods 80 years hence.

Dr Pepper thus joins ranks with a select group of products that point to the 1904 World's Fair and Exposition where the theme song "Meet Me in St. Louie, Louie" was an invitation to some 20,000,000 visitors to enjoy products that were new on the scene but have since become part of American tradition.

The City of St. Louis has lived up to its enviable heritage and in 1965 erected a remarkable landmark to commemorate its historic role as Gateway to the West. They named it "The Gateway Arch" — magnificent engineering achievement and a symbol of American progress that rises 630 feet high along the Mississippi River to become the nation's tallest monument.

* *History of Louisiana Purchase Exposition from Adair's New Encyclopedia, copyright 1923-1924.*
* *Athens, Texas Chamber of Commerce and excerpts from Frank Tolbert's historical Texas writings.*
* *Saint Louis University, Public Relations Department.*

"DR PEPPER—KING OF BEVERAGES"

Shortly following Dr Pepper's origin in 1885, R. S. Lazenby founded the Artesian Manufacturing & Bottling Company which would produce and sell the new drink. The company initially began operations in a building located at 327 S. Fifth Street in Waco, Texas. Lazenby had previously established the Circle "A" Corporation of America to produce and sell his Circle "A" Ginger Ale, a high quality drink that had achieved considerable success. Records indicate that both companies operated from this location.

Not wanting to abandon his highly successful Circle "A" Company, Lazenby created a second to bottle and sell his Dr Pepper's Phos-Ferrates along with other flavored soft drinks including Wine Cola, Celery Champagne and Zu Zu fruit drinks.

Another of his unique products at the time was Aqua Lithia, a purified mineral water drawn from his 1,890 foot artesian well which he had drilled directly beneath his new bottling plant building.

Lazenby, if not the first, was one of the first to bottle and sell water in the U.S. under the name "Aqua Lithia" which was advertised under its own label. It was remarkable that he could sell his bottled water since Waco, at the time, acquired its entire water supply from twenty deep artesian wells that had been drilled within its city limits. City records show these wells averaged 1,800 feet or more in depth and that Waco became known as "The City of Wells." Cutter, in his 1904 Almanac, called Waco "The Geyser City" and described it as a popular health resort. Many people came to Waco to enjoy mineral water baths. The water that came from the wells emerged at 106 degrees and under high pressure.

Dr Pepper soon proved to be a "comer" for Lazenby. He began to recognize its potential as an out-of-the-ordinary soft drink. This prompted him to begin special advertising and promotion on Dr Pepper. He was not one without imagination and his English ancestry, like that of many of his contemporaries, made him familiar with the early development of carbonated drinks.

Dr Pepper's Phos-Ferrates, Aqua Lithia (bottled water), and Artesian Soda were main line products of the Artesian Manufacturing & Bottling Company prior to 1900.

In 1886, Robert S. Lazenby, in partnership with Wade B. Morrison, founded the Artesian Mfg. & Bottling Co., in Waco, Texas and established operations in this building at 327 S. Fifth Street where Dr Pepper was first bottled.

Carbonated waters originated in England. Although a number of men were involved, Dr. Joseph Priestly, prominent English scientist, played a major role in this early development. It was Priestly who first discovered how to produce carbonated water artificially back in 1772, by impregnating water with air. He published his directions for this process in London, describing what he called "Pyrmont Water" and other mineral waters of familiar nature.

Other prominent English authorities are credited with further research and study on mineral and carbonated waters including Dr. Joseph Black, at the University of Edinburgh, and Thomas Cooper who later became one of America's pioneeer industrial chemists.

In view of this extensive English influence in the development of carbonated drinks, it was only to be expected that Lazenby would seek to identify his Dr Pepper with this background.

Dr Pepper had met with great favor among those who tried it since its initial introduction at Morrison's Old Corner Drug. Wanting to enhance its image and acceptance, Lazenby sought to

R. S. Lazenby, founder of Dr Pepper Company, was aware of the major role of English scientists in the origin of carbonated drinks. This led him to use a full-color print of King George the Fifth in a poster and the slogan, "Dr Pepper–King of Beverages."

find a prestigious medium on which to base his advertising and promotion. He judiciously chose to relate it back to the English and their prominent role in the origin and development of carbonated drinks.

Using this premise what could be more appropriate than to identify somehow with the King of England himself? Lazenby's first Dr Pepper poster advertisement was a full color print reproduction of King George the Fifth. Embossed at the top of the print was "Dr Pepper - King of Beverages . . . at Fountains and in Bottles."

Apparently this was the only advertisement using a picture of the King, but Lazenby's ingenuity would not be denied. Concerned that he not demean the King, he then used the next more prominent English symbol which was a full-color painting of a lion. It not only identified with the King but denoted strength and dignity.

So it was, "King of Beverages" and the lion became the Dr Pepper symbol. The first major advertisement using the lion appeared on a thirty-foot wall sign on a building in downtown

Waco in early 1900. Painted by Louis Sternkorb, the lion art was used extensively to advertise Dr Pepper up until 1920.

The lion also was used as deco art on plates, printed promotional materials and in newspaper and magazine advertisements. "Dr Pepper - King of Beverages" like many historic advertising slogans, traces back to the origin of the drink and was used as an appendage for some twenty years.

No one can say the "Dr Pepper - King of Beverages" slogan was coincidence. Lazenby thoughtfully created it from his own thorough knowledge and appreciation of the English involvement in the development of carbonated drinks which have become a worldwide industry. It was his way to recognize this origin and capitalize on it in a dignified way.

"Dr Pepper - King of Beverages," celebrating its 100th Anniversary in 1985, is indebted to R. S. Lazenby for many things, but most of all, for his confidence that Dr Pepper would indeed be a product of long vintage. He must likewise receive credit for his recognition of individuals who have shared in the founding of a product and a company that has survived in a highly competitive industry for more than 100 years.

THE MAN WHO PUT "POP" IN SODA POP

From out of posterity comes recognition that is justly due a man who launched the tide of economic history for one of the great industries in America. We're speaking of Dr. Joseph Priestly, self-educated English scientist and theologian and the multi-billion dollar carbonated soft drink industry.

Some forty years ago, in 1945, Dr Pepper Company duly acknowledged Priestly when J. B. O'Hara, then president of the

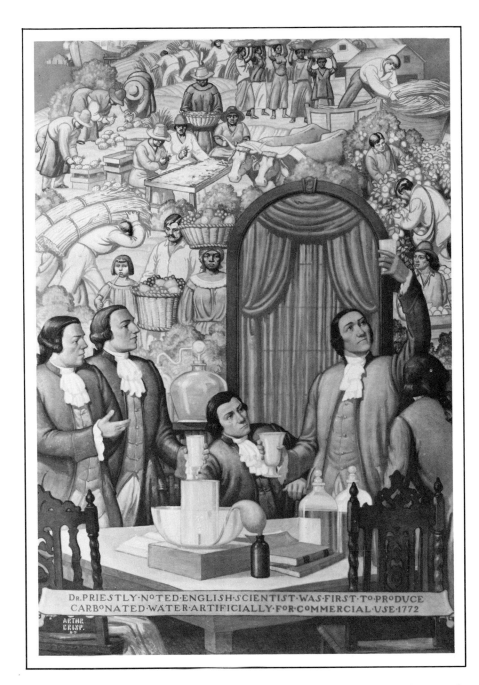

Dr. Joseph Priestly, English scientist, was first to discover the process for producing carbonated water artificially. This illustration, from a 12-foot mural in the Dr Pepper Company lobby in Dallas, was done by Arthur Crisp, prominent New York muralist, in 1948 along with three others depicting the history of carbonated drinks.

company, authorized Arthur Crisp, prominent New York muralist, to do a series of four paintings depicting the origin and history of carbonated soft drinks. In the mural depicting their origin, Priestly is the central figure, appropriately so because of his discovery of oxygen.

O'Hara conducted an extensive search to find the right artist to do the murals and finally selected Crisp, Canadian born artist whose credits were impressive and included the First Hallgareta prize from the National Academy of Design, 1916, and numerous other national and international awards.

Crisp spent many months researching the origin and history of carbonated waters and beverages before starting the paintings. His target date for completion was 1948, when Dr Pepper Company would move into its new multi-million dollar offices and

Joseph Priestley
USA 20c

U.S. Postage Stamp celebrates man who put "POP" in soda pop. On April 13, 1983, 210 years after his discovery of oxygen, a U.S. Postage stamp was issued in honor of Joseph Priestly, prominent English scientist. Priestly and his British contemporaries played a major role in the development of carbonated water.

manufacturing facility located at Mockingbird and Greenville in Dallas. The 6' X 12' murals were to be the center attraction in the main lobby of the new facility. Since the murals were installed in 1948, they have become recognized for their historical significance and Dr. Joseph Priestly is a prominent figure in these artistic portrayals of the history of carbonated beverages.

It was especially appropriate that the U.S. Postal Service produced a commemorative stamp to mark the 250th Anniversary of Priestly's birth. The appropriateness of the stamp is soundly justified. The multi-billion dollar carbonated beverage industry that flourishes not only in the U.S., but in most countries around the world today, is indeed monumental evidence of the magnitude of his discovery.

Priestly was born near Leeds in England in 1733 and studied for the ministry. He lectured in Suffolk for several years on history and the sciences. Finally he became a dissenting, nonconformist minister in Leeds and Birmingham.

Through his friendship with Benjamin Franklin, he became interested in electricity, and together they performed many brilliant experiments. In 1772 he turned to chemistry discovering hydrochloric acid and laughing gas (nitrous oxide). In 1774 he discovered sulfur dioxide.

The 18th century British chemist and theologian, who is perhaps best known as the "father of oxygen," never had any formal training in science. It was by accident that he discovered carbon dioxide while researching the gas he had produced from fermenting grain. His increasing involvement in alchemy led to his greatest discovery—oxygen in 1774.

Priestly designated the new colorless, odorless and tasteless gas "dephlogisticated air" because of its combustion characteristics. Antoine Lavoister renamed the gas "Oxygen."

Priestly began his experiments with "fixed air" in 1767, including attempts to combine it with water to simulate natural spring water. This he did in a brewery in Leeds, using the gas over fermenting vats. With the water absorbing the gas, his initial method involved pouring water from one vessel to another, both being held as near as possible to the yeast fermentation.

In 1772 he published his results for impregnating water with fixed air and was recognized as the first to produce carbonated water artificially. It was in 1772, also, that Priestly presented his paper entitled "Observations on Different Kinds of Air" before the Royal Society of London.

For Priestly's contribution to science through his studies concerning "fixed air" and combining it with liquids, emphasizing that water impregnated with carbon dioxide would prevent sea scurvy, and should be useful for that purpose in medicine, he was awarded the Copley Medal in 1773 by the Royal Society.

One of Priestly's strongly-expressed religious opinions caused a public furor when it was published in his "History of the Corruptions of Christianity," in 1782.

After a mob destroyed Priestly's church, home and laboratory, he fled England and sought asylum in Northumberland, Pennsylvania.

Although Priestly is better known for his influence in the field of science, during the last decade of his life in America theology played a more predominant role. He lectured and wrote extensively during that period on topics principally theological in nature.

Dickinson College, founded in 1773 in Carlisle, Pennsylvania, has long been interested in Dr. Joseph Priestly and his contributions to the development of chemical research. Through Thomas Cooper, distinguished member of the Dickinson faculty in the early 19th Century, most of the original apparatus belonging to Priestly became the property of the College and has been preserved as a tangible link with his discovery of oxygen.

The Priestly Museum in Northumberland, Pennsylvania, is another tribute to the man who is credited with one of the most important discoveries in the history of science.

So the 1985 20¢ U.S. Postage Stamp commemorating the 250th Anniversary of Priestly's birth deserves special recognition, particularly among the thousands of people who go to make up one of the most successful and visible industries in the world—the producers of carbonated beverages.

It bears significance also in light of the fact that carbonated soft drinks have become synonomous with the way of life for millions of people around the world. No other product is more closely identified with the personal habits of so many people.

After all—it was Dr. Joseph Priestly (1733 - 1804) who put the "pop" in these products and zest in life for the past 250 years.

"DRINK A BITE TO EAT AT 10-2-AND 4 O'CLOCK"

VICTOR HUGO, well known French author, wrote in 1852 "Greater than the tread of mighty armies is an idea whose time has come." Hugo's writings clearly indicate that he was a man of ideas, having coined a few that far outlived him. He is probably best known as the author of "The Hunchback of Notre Dame," a novel that has been filmed, satirized, dramatized and copied in text for the enjoyment and entertainment of people around the world for the past 100 years.

Hugo, who died in 1885, the year Dr Pepper was born, would never know that ninety-nine years later his loveable Hunchback would spark an idea for a Dr Pepper TV commercial.

In the 100-year history of Dr Pepper, ideas have been the spark for much of its progress. One, whose time came in the late twenties and refuses to go away, was "Drink a Bite to Eat at 10 - 2 - & 4 O'clock." What makes it even more interesting and unusual is the story of its origin.

World War II had just begun and the United States was caught up in it in a big way. It was also caught short of armaments and munitions and the entire nation was frantically trying to catch up with the dire demands.

Explosives were one of the critically short items and sugar was the principal ingredient in their production. This prompted the U.S. Government to issue an order restricting the use of sugar to essential items only. Soft drinks did not qualify by the government classification, even though there were thousands of soft drink bottle vendors dispensing their products in war production plants employing thousands of workers. They were being pushed to capacity on all fronts.

J. B. O'Hara, chairman of the board of Dr Pepper Company, was acutely aware of all this and also that soft drinks containing sugar provided a "quick energy boost." He reasoned that these large numbers of war plant workers, in order to produce at maximum levels, would benefit by consuming soft drinks during their work

The "Drink a Bite to Eat" slogan gave consumers a reason to drink Dr Pepper at the hours of 10, 2 and 4 o'clock. It became the most penetrating advertising slogan ever used by Dr Pepper Company.

break periods. But he needed more convincing evidence than his own since he was, after all, head of a large soft drink company.

Like his predecessor, R. S. Lazenby, who founded the company, O'Hara was a man of lofty ideas. He deplored the "sins" of contemporary members of the carbonated beverage industry during the era in which soft drinks had acquired the popular but none too complimentary nickname "soda pop."

He insisted that Dr Pepper was a food in liquid form, deserved professional and public respect and aspired to achieve recognition of its proper value and place in the daily diet. Incidentally, O'Hara did not realize that some years later there would be scientific support for between-meal snacks from no less an authority than Dr. Haggard of Yale University.

O'Hara persisted in his idea and finally went to Dr. Walter H. Eddy, pH.D and eminent professor of Physiological Chemistry at Columbia University in New York who was nationally recognized as an authority on nutrition and vitamins. O'Hara described the situation and arranged with Dr. Eddy to conduct thorough research on daily human fatigue.

After extensive study and experiments, Dr. Eddy discovered that the average person experienced a normal letdown in energy at the hours of 10:30, 2:30 and 4:30. He learned that the blood sugar dropped to its lowest level at these periods and reasoned that an intake of sugar would restore energy to the normal level.

Encouraged by Dr. Eddy's findings, O'Hara went to the War Rationing Board in Washington with his new evidence and a proposal that soft drinks continue to be made available to war plant workers, thus helping them maintain work levels at peak performance. He contended that soft drinks provided a suitable energy lift for workers when they needed it.

After viewing the evidence the Rationing Board agreed that it was sound and immediately rescinded their order, allowing carbonated drinks a sugar quota, 90% of which would be available for war plant employees. This action not only proved beneficial to the war effort, but saved the soft drink industry from being completely closed down during the war years of 1944–1947.

O'Hara and his company as far back as 1927 had pioneered the idea that Dr Pepper be classified as a food since between-meal supplemental feeding was recognized not only as desirable but a vital factor in public health, morale and physical efficiency. But

Earl Racey coined the Dr Pepper slogan, "Drink a Bite to Eat at 10 - 2 & 4 O'Clock" to win the $25 prize.

The 10-2-4 Clock Dial emblem became a popular trademark emblem used in Dr Pepper advertising for more than thirty years. It still serves as the title for the Company's national news publication.

not until Dr. Eddy conducted his study was he able to support his dietary theory about soft drinks and Dr Pepper.

Not one to sleep on an idea, O'Hara took it to his advertising agency, Tracy-Locke-Dawson, Inc., of Dallas and suggested they seek appropriate ways to promote it. Raymond P. Locke, president of the agency, called his staff together to explore the possibilities. After presenting all the facts, he concluded the meeting by offering a $25 bonus to any member for an acceptable advertising slogan for Dr Pepper.

A week passed and nothing had impressed Locke until late on Friday afternoon when Earl Racey walked into his office and dropped a slip of paper on his desk. Locke picked it up and read, "Drink a Bite to Eat at 10- 2- & 4 O'Clock."

Racey stood silent and finally Locke spoke, "Racey, you've done it. I knew that $25 would produce results."

Neither Locke nor Racey at the time realized what a bargain idea they had. It marked the beginning of a bold new advertising concept, not only for Dr Pepper but for other soft drinks as well. Dr Pepper pioneered the idea that soft drinks be classified as a food and launched a campaign featuring its drink in the food supplement category which lasted for some twenty years. It consistently led the industry in promoting soft drinks as "energy food." In conjunction with "Drink a Bite to Eat at 10 - 2 & 4 O'Clock," came such advertising slogans as "Energy Up," "Energy Lift," and "Pepper-Upper."

But nothing ever quite matched Racey's original slogan idea. The company adopted a second registered trademark to be used in concert with its original logo in the form of a clock dial featuring three hands pointing to the numerals 10, 2 and 4.

Soft drink companies over the years have made prolific use of slogans but research has shown that Dr Pepper's 10 - 2 & 4 slogan dominated them all. It was not until 1940 when Benton & Bowles replaced Tracy-Locke as Dr Pepper's ad agency that the 10-2-4 slogan was beginning to be replaced. Even then, Benton & Bowles did not recommend that it be dropped; they simply gave it a new twist and said, "Three Good Times to Enjoy Life More."

Today, some forty years since Racey coined his winning Dr Pepper slogan, it continues to attract interest. Each year the company receives numerous inquiries about its origin and meaning. Consumer research has repeatedly indicated that "Drink a Bite to Eat at 10 - 2 & 4 O'Clock" was one of the most penetrating advertising lines ever used. It aroused interest, it has a curious appeal and most important of all, it was based on sound reasoning. It is an idea that won't go away!

The first shot of "Shoot a Waco" was fired at Morrison's Old Corner Drug which became both an institution and a landmark in Waco, Texas. Not only as the birthplace of Dr Pepper, it was also renowned for dispensing medicinal cures for ailments of both man and beast. The Old Corner Drug was also a communications center, the place to leave and receive messages and a source of news of important current events.

During the war, letters from servicemen with "news from the front" were posted in the store. Morrison's Old Corner Drug was a pivotal center in Waco in its heyday but it earned its prominence as "The Birthplace of Dr Pepper."

The first shot of "Shoot a Waco" was not heard around the world at the time, but one hundred years later it is being heard throughout much of it including Europe, Africa, Japan, The Middle and Far East.

"SHOOT A WACO"

If you're not too young, "Shoot a Waco" may ring familiar and bring back some pleasant memories. A few short years ago, when corner drug stores just about dominated prominent street intersections in every town and city, "Shoot a Waco" was common jargon among the scores of young soda jerks.

Soda jerks, for the benefit of the too young, were the young men who dispensed carbonated soft drinks and other taste-tempting delights at these corner drug soda fountains.

"Shoot a Waco" was the adopted sobriquet of these young dispensers in ordering Dr Pepper. It became so familiar that fountain customers themselves often used the term for Dr Pepper.

All the way from Waco to Dallas to St. Louis, Chicago, Atlanta,

Denver and places in between people were aware that Dr Pepper originated in Waco, Texas. The name of the drink had become infixed with the name of the city where it originated, and some fountain patrons weren't sure which was which.

This was no fluke identity. Those who know about Dr Pepper know of its unique relationship with Waco since it was first introduced there in 1885. One hundred years later this relationship has only grown deeper; a situation that is both unique and enviable among commercial products.

Waco itself is as unique and out-of-the-ordinary as Dr Pepper. One native Wacoan said it was as if they were destined to be a part of each other. History suggests Waco was the right place for Dr Pepper to begin and that Dr Pepper was the right product to have its origin in this Central Texas city.

From the beginning there were parallels in the nature and character of Waco and Dr Pepper. Both were germane in ways that would grow through the years. The people of Waco were explicit in their political, social and religious views. There was never any doubt about their position on important issues and much the same is true today.

Dr Pepper is an explicit flavored soft drink, distinct and never confused with any other. The people of Waco and Dr Pepper still bear similar distinctions they have enjoyed over the years, even though Waco has grown from a small village on the banks of the Brazos River to a city of over 100,000 people and Dr Pepper has grown to be one of the leading American soft drinks with distribution throughout the entire U.S. and in many foreign countries.

The heritage of Waco goes far beyond its founding in 1850. It is the seat of McLennan County and the centermost city in Texas. Many tribes of Indians inhabited the area long before white settlers arrived. The strong attraction of the fertile Brazos River Valley resulted in the formation of a new tribe of Indians which became known as the Huacos. Historians indicate they were a mixture of the Tawakonis, the Wichitas and the Caddos from East Texas.

For more than a thousand years before the arrival of Columbus, many tribes of Indians lived, hunted and farmed along the Brazos. Their strong influence would not be erased and became a part of the culture of early Waco.

Dr Pepper entered the scene just as the city was beginning to establish its own image apart from its long Indian heritage. The white settlers had won out and Waco was no longer the Indian village on the banks of the Brazos. The new Waco was a mixture of Spanish, French, Mexican and American which produced a wide diversity of citizens in the community. They had difficulty, even to the spelling of the city name which came from the Indian tribe of Wacos. Early documents show there were thirty different spellings of the name.

The man who is heralded as the city's founder is Major George B. Erath, an Austrian who had fled military service in his country at the age of 15. He migrated to the United States and first lived in Alabama, moving to Texas when he was barely 20.

Erath was highly educated and a young man of great vision. His leadership in establishing Waco as a Texas crossroads city is legend with the founding of the west and as epical as anything on record concerning the great American pioneer adventure.

Dr Pepper was fortunate to be a part of this heritage. Its origin was as if planned to have a part in the Waco scenario. From the beginning, when Dr Pepper first entered the scene, it was on center stage in Waco. It started out as a product of high quality and out-of-the-ordinary taste. It came at a time when Wacoans were looking for out-of-the-ordinary ways and means to expand their city.

Dr Pepper, as a home-grown product, met with favor on its first serving at Morrison's Old Corner Drug Store. It offered bragging rights to the city developers which they have celebrated continuously over the years. R. S. Lazenby, the man who perfected Dr Pepper's formula, became one of the city's prominent citizens. His reputation as a beverage chemist, his business leadership and his keen insight into the affairs of the city made him a key figure in Waco.

The early success of Dr Pepper indicated that it was not a "flash in the glass" at Morrison's fountain. As its popularity increased, other fountain operators in Waco began buying the flavoring syrup and serving the drink, thus marking the beginning of a truly American original which has continued its success over a period of 100 years.

But what about the distinctions that are synonymous with Waco and Dr Pepper? In looking back, there were events and situations that seem to be made to order for both. Baylor University, one of the great institutions of higher learning not only in Texas but in America, is located in Waco. It was founded in 1845 under charter from the Republic of Texas by James Huckins, William M. Tryon and Robert E. B. Baylor, for whom the university was named. The school bears many distinctions, one of which is the Baylor bear, mascot of its football team, which has an affinity for Dr Pepper. This has been true with each of the 42 bears that have performed in this role.

Was it coincidence that the Baylor mascot was a bear which traditionally is known to have a sweet tooth, and coincidence that Dr Pepper was a perfect sweet tooth appeaser?

Waco began suffering from growth pains early. Its leaders were enterprising and recognized the great potential of the city. The Brazos River had been a formidable barrier to travelers moving west and the primary crossing was by ferry. It was a natural challenge for Wacoans to be the first to erect a bridge across the Brazos where travelers would not have to ferry or ford the often deep and treacherous river.

A unique and rare art piece in the Dr Pepper archives is a limited edition of Baylor "Pepper" Pride, a 9 1/2" bronze sculpture of the Baylor University Bear mascot by Don Hunt. What makes it unique and special is the history of the mascot's long patronage of Dr Pepper which helps control his behavior. Hunt's work defines a new tradition in bronze sculpture. A student of Randy Steffen, he devoted painstaking research for detail and accuracy. Baylor "Pepper" Pride presents the bear with his favorite soft drink and the craftsmanship of the artist.

In 1870 Waco celebrated the completion of a wire cable suspension bridge, an engineering achievement and one of the longest single span suspension bridges in the world. It stands today as a majestic landmark to the city of Waco.

Commemorate art plate featuring the Texas Cotton Palace, produced by R. S. Lazenby, compliments of his Circle "A" Ginger Ale.

The completion of the ALICO building by the Amicable Life Insurance Co., in Waco, Texas triggered a Prosperity Banquet celebration on April 10, 1911. On April 25, 1985 it was at the center of a repeat Prosperity Banquet by Wacoans, celebrating Dr Pepper's 100th anniversary in Waco.

On January 6, 1870, the city celebrated completion of a wire cable suspension bridge, erected by John A. Roebling & Son, the same firm that had built the Brooklyn Bridge. It was an engineering achievement and one of the longest single-span suspension bridges in the world.

Dr Pepper had come on the scene soon afterward and was now ready to become a major participant in Waco history. In 1906 the Artesian Manufacturing & Bottling Co., forerunner to Dr Pepper Company, completed construction of its own impressive new building to become "The Home of Dr Pepper." Located at 5th and Mary, only a short distance from the campus of Baylor University, the three-story Romanesque style building was hailed as another major achievement in the business enterprise of Waco. Walls of the building were 14″ solid brick with steel and concrete foundation.

Directly beneath the building Lazenby drilled an 1,800′ artesian well which provided pure sparkling water for the bottling of Dr Pepper and other private label soft drinks.

"The Home of Dr Pepper" in Waco received industry-wide acclaim which added credibility to Waco's bragging rights as the Texas Crossroads City.

In the civic and business life of Waco, Dr Pepper has been conspicuously involved since its origin 100 years ago. In 1911 the city celebrated completion of a 22-story skyscraper building, home of the Amicable Life Insurance Co. It was publicized as the tallest building west of the Mississippi River and received national attention.

To celebrate their new building, plus the extension of the Cotton Belt and Santa Fe Railroads to provide service to Waco, the Young Men's Business League, which later became the Waco Chamber of Commerce, sponsored a "Prosperity Banquet" which was held on the streets of downtown Waco adjacent to the new building.

Held on April 10, 1911, it was an auspicious occasion with all of the city leaders present along with numerous visiting dignitaries, totaling some 2,000 guests.

R. S. Lazenby was deeply involved in the affair, and one of his contributions to the banquet was a complimentary bottle of Dr Pepper at the plate of each dinner guest.

Completion of the new building had other significant effects on downtown Waco and attracted new business to the area. Its modern new facilities were not overlooked by Wade Morrison, proprietor and owner of the Old Corner Drug Store where Dr Pepper had been introduced fifteen years earlier. Morrison moved the store from its 4th and Austin corner location into the new Amicable building, modernizing its features in keeping with the new quarters.

The list of credits and achievements of Waco has multiplied over the years. It was celebrated as the Cotton Capital of the Southwest and attracted buyers for the product from around the world. Each year the harvest was celebrated in grandiose manner with a colorful pageant and coronation ball held in the magnificent Cotton Palace, a great hall that would accommodate 10,000 guests.

To commemorate the Texas Cotton Palace, Lazenby produced a beautiful art deco plate, compliments of his Circle "A" Ginger Ale. Today the plate is a valuable "collectible" artifact.

Cattle drivers charted their route north through Waco where cowpokes celebrated their stop in customary style which caused the city to become known as "Six-Shooter Junction."

This was one of a number of monikers the city acquired for various and dubious reasons. As the 19th century gave way to the 20th, Waco grew in population, changing from an agricultural economy to an industrial center. It became known as "The Athens of Texas," a cultural and educational center for the State. Another title for Waco was "The Geyser City," coming from its status as a health resort based on the area's abundant mineral waters.

Like other pioneer cities of the west, Waco met up with its share of lawlessness. The constant melees between cattle drivers, Indians and settlers led Stephen F. Austin to organize a group of volunteers to range over the area between the Colorado and Brazos Rivers. These men became known as the Texas Rangers and early in 1837, Texas Secretary of War, William S. Fisher, ordered a company of Rangers to build a fort at Waco Indian Village. It became known as Fort Fisher and a refuge from unruly invaders.

Fort Fisher is now one of Texas' most popular museums, housing a wealth of artifacts and Texas Ranger memorabilia.

As Waco moved into the twentieth century it became a center of more contemporary military activities. It is surrounded by three important service bases operated by the U.S. Government; Camp Arthur, established during World War I, the Waco Army Air Field in World War II, and Fort Hood, a major army training base opened in 1942.

Waco experienced all the struggles and dangers that came with the territory of the early west, and has the scars to show for it. It produced men of great courage and character whose names fill the pages of Texas history.

Dr Pepper was a part of this Waco drama and its mark is indelibly stamped on the city. No one there now orders Dr Pepper with "Shoot A Waco" but the population has never let up ordering it. The Waco franchise market has ranked number one in Dr Pepper per capita sales 18 out of the past 38 years and today's Wacoans are the fifth generation of Dr Pepper drinkers.

One thing has not changed, Wacoans are still "Shooting a Waco" even though they no longer ask for it by this long popular soda jerk's jargon.

Throughout 1985 large portable signs reminded Wacoans and visitors to the city that Waco is the home of Dr Pepper which was celebrating its 100 Original Years.

This Artesia Bottling Co. delivery wagon was an "attention getter" and so was the painted wall sign featuring the Company's leading soft drink.

A Dr Pepper Legend

ARTESIA BOTTLING COMPANY FORT WORTH, TEXAS

Fort Worth, Texas traditionally is referred to as "Cowtown – where the West begins." It is likewise one of the cities where Dr Pepper had its early beginning. Fort Worth became the first location outside of Waco where Dr Pepper was bottled.

The Artesia Bottling Company that opened there in 1905 was an offshoot of the original Waco operation founded in 1885 by Robert S. Lazenby. It was perceptible that one of his brothers, Henry Lazenby, would become the Forth Worth manager.

The company started doing business at 316-318 Kentucky Avenue at the corner of Henryetta. A Fort Worth city directory advertisement, published in 1905, listed the company's products as Dr Peppers's Phos Ferrates, ZU ZU Ginger Ale, Celery Champagne and Big A soda flavors.

Well in advance of motorized vehicles, the mode of delivery for soft drinks was strictly by horse and wagon. Like his brother, Henry Lazenby prided himself in his beautiful horses and delivery wagons. The wagons, with 44-case capacity, were custom made by the Reliable Carriage Works of Fort Worth and carried dominant signs advertising his products.

Dr Pepper was off to a good start in Fort Worth, only ninety miles to the north of Waco where people were well acquainted with the new drink. The business grew rapidly and in 1908 a larger brick building was erected at 1315 East Front Street to handle the increased volume. Not long afterward this facility was enlarged by the addition of a second floor.

Henry Lazenby was a smooth talker and a good salesman but

Three views of the original Artesia Bottling Co., quarters in Fort Worth show the excellent growth of the business which prompted the changes.

An original bottle used by the Artesia Bottling Co. dating back to early 1900, is today considered highly collectible.

not too level headed and a poor businessman. He had many heated run-ins with those he dealt with, one of which led to a serious argument that resulted in his being shot and killed. It happened on Wednesday, June 5, 1918.

Ed Ratliff had worked as a salesman for Lazenby for two weeks. On the morning of June 5, he had words with Lazenby over a truck he had been driving. The argument led to a scuffle and Lazenby ran to his upstairs office where he had a gun.

Ratliff left the plant and went to his home. Around noon he returned with his gun to collect $8.40 in salary Lazenby still owed him. As he walked into Lazenby's office, Lazenby was seated in his revolving chair at his desk. As Ratliff spoke, Lazenby suddenly opened a desk drawer and pulled out his revolver. He stood up and aimed at Ratliff who lunged forward to grab the gun.

Lazenby got off one shot which grazed Ratliff's hand. By then Ratliff had pulled his own gun which he fired one time. The bullet struck Lazenby in the head and he slumped back down into his chair.

Ratliff took both guns and walked about half a block down the street where he called the police. The shot proved fatal for Lazenby. He remained in critical condition until June 18 when he died from the wound.

Ironically, Henry Lazenby's nature and character was much like that of his brother Robert who often clashed with others during business dealings.

Following the tragedy, Henry's wife, Georgiana Polster Lazenby, along with her brother, George, ran the company. Also joining them was Donald H. Wiley who moved up from Waco to help manage the business. Too much had gone wrong, however, and the business floundered. In 1919 it was taken over by W. C. Guffey and W. J. Hefley who also owned and operated an ice cream business. They combined the two businesses and it became known as the Artesia Bottling and Ice Cream Co.

Two years later Guffey and Hefley dissolved their partnership. Guffey and D. P. Berry opened The Acme Bottling Works to produce Delaware Punch which they thought would become the big seller.

Hefley took another partner, E. T. Renfro, who, at the time, was proprietor of several drug stores in Fort Worth which later grew into a large chain operation.

Around 1921 Hefley pulled out of the company leaving Renfro the sole owner. Renfro hired a manager for the business, still operating as the Artesia Bottling Co., but after two years decided it was a loser and closed it down. Afterward he discovered the manager was mishandling the company funds and that it could have been a profitable business.

In spite of these reverses, Dr Pepper had made sales inroads in the Fort Worth market. In order to maintain this business, the Dr Pepper Bottling Co. of Dallas began serving the area.

In 1928 H. B. Dorris, who had worked as bookkeeper and general manager for R. S. Lazenby in Waco, was issued a Dr Pepper franchise agreement for the Forth Worth market. This marked the beginning of a long and successful Dr Pepper bottling operation serving Fort Worth.

H. B. Dorris was joined by his brother, W. F. Dorris, and later by his two sons, H. B., Jr., and W. L. They pooled their experiences to build the company into one of the most successful bottling operations in Texas. By the mid-thirties, Dr Pepper sales had outstripped their production capacity and in 1938 the company completed a new plant at 1401 Henderson Avenue, rated by many as a model bottling facility. Sparkling with all new stainless steel equipment, it became a "showcase operation."

A special feature of the new plant was a handsome clock tower

equipped with carillon bells that chimed on the hour denoting the time.

Needless to say, the new plant and its attendant publicity brought added prestige and increased business to the firm.

A fourth partner in the Fort Worth operation who played a major role in its early success was W. Gaines Sparks who started working part time while still attending school. In 1936 Sparks became a full-time employee and in 1943, when the Fort Worth owners purchased the Dr Pepper Bottling Company of Rockford, Illinois, Sparks moved there to serve as manager until the plant was sold in 1950.

Sparks returned to Fort Worth to become vice president, secretary and treasurer, holding this position until 1960 when he became president.

Tragedy in the meantime had taken a heavy toll among the Dorris family. The untimely death at age 39 from a heart attack on December 30, 1950, of H. B. Dorris, Jr., marked the beginning. Four months later, on April 23, 1951, the tragedy repeated itself at the death of H. B. Dorris, Sr., the man who had piloted the company from a meager beginning to a million $ business.

The third member of the Dorris management team and young-est son of H. B. Dorris, Sr., W. L. "Brownie" Dorris, took over the reins of the company. Like his father and brother, "Brownie" followed the same basics of operation that had proved successful for Dr Pepper in the Fort Worth market for many years.

Ironically, however, the younger Dorris was denied the opportunity to share in the fruits of long efforts of his family. On August 16, 1959, W. L. Dorris, at the age of 35, suffered the same malady that had taken his father and older brother only a few short years earlier.

Thus it remained for W. Gaines Sparks, brother-in-law to H. B. Dorris, Sr., to manage the company. Sparks, with his 33 years of service with the company, was well prepared for the job. He simply picked up where his predecessors left off and continued to run the business as before. This is not to say he was without valuable assistance from other veteran employees also well grounded in the company's policies and programs. One of these in particular was W. F. Estill, vice president and sales manager for the company. Estill began his employment with the company back in his 'teens working for Guffey and Hefley in 1919.

Despite the tragic losses the company had experienced, Dr Pepper sales in Fort Worth climbed steadily over the years. Volume continued to exceed production and on December 4, 1965, the company moved into a brand new $600,000 plant located at 201 East Felix Street. Like the previous facility, except ten times enlarged, it represented the latest in bottling plant operations. Although not privileged to be present to enjoy the occasion, it was a glowing tribute to H. B. Dorris, Sr., and his family who had laid solid groundwork for the company.

In 1965 the Dr Pepper Bottling Company of Fort Worth moved into this modern new facility located at 201 East Felix Street.

One would have to feel that the Fort Worth business had more than its share of reverses through the untimely death of its managers, but there was more to come. After some twenty years of sharing in the management of the company, Sparks, like his predecessors, was stricken and, following a short illness, died on December 3, 1967.

The Fort Worth story at this point should have a sequel which would read as though it had been pre-written for success. Following all of the tireless and dedicated effort of H. B. Dorris, Sr., his two sons, H. B. and W. L., and his brother-in-law, Sparks, a conclusion would be they had been cheated out of hard earned rewards.

Since 1928 the company had continually moved forward in sales and earnings. The sequel was H. B. Dorris, III, grandson of the company founder, who now stepped into the leadership role. Fortunately again, young Dorris had gained his experience from "growing up" in the business plus valuable help from Estill and the other veteran employees as well as a brother-in-law Don Sanford who had joined the company.

Although relatively young, they matured rapidly in their responsibility and carried on the affairs of the business in a highly professional way to maintain the momentum which had marked success for Dr Pepper in Fort Worth. Other members of the Dorris family shared in the operation of the business, especially during the critical periods of transition, one in particular, Margaret (Dorris) Blanton, daughter of the founder, who served as secretary and treasurer.

By 1970, Fort Worth and Dallas had grown together to become a giant metro market. Closeness and compactness of the two cities resulted in overlapping of advertising and marketing programs as well as some conflicts where they did not encompass the total area.

In 1973, the Fort Worth Dr Pepper Bottling Co., negotiated to sell its interest to Dr Pepper Company which owned the Dallas franchise. This merged the two markets into one metroplex operation serving both cities with a combined population of some 3,000,000 people.

The Fort Worth and Dallas merger opened an important new chapter in Dr Pepper history in North Texas and one that continues to offer unlimited potential. The merger is indicative of the trend that has marked the progress of Dr Pepper and soft drinks

Founders of the Artesia Bottling Co., of Fort Worth could be proud that their early struggles and dedication to Dr Pepper would result in outstanding success. In 1980 the Dr Pepper Metroplex Refreshment Company, serving Fort Worth and Dallas, moved its operations into this twenty million dollar facility in Irving, Texas, midway between the two cities. It is one of the largest soft drink bottling and canning operations in North America.

generally during the past decade. It also presages a movement that promises further change for soft drink bottlers in the future.

The latest chapter concerning the Fort Worth –Dallas Dr Pepper bottling operation transpired in February 1985 when the Dr Pepper Company, in its financial divestment program, sold the business to Hicks & Haas, a Dallas merchant banking firm. One of the principals in the transaction was Jim L. Turner, president of the Dallas/Fort Worth operation, who would continue to serve as president under the new ownership. Included in the sale was the Dr Pepper Bottling Company of Waco where Dr Pepper had its historic origin in 1885.

Dr Pepper was first bottled by the Artesian Mfg. & Bottling Co., with product identification appearing on the crown. Size of the bottles varied, averaging from 8 to 10 ounces and the shape changed frequently.

DR PEPPER PACKAGING PARADE

Necessity may have been the mother of invention but it was always accompanied by a challenge to produce a better mousetrap that would bring improvement and change.

Speaking of change, nowhere can we find a better example than from the history of products and packaging in the soft drink industry. Carbonated beverage history began at the soda fountain where drinks were first served in glass tumblers. They were called tumblers because drinks were poured from one glass to another to promote effervescence. Charles Alderton, the originator of Dr Pepper, dispensed his first drink in a glass tumbler in 1885.

Bottles were already being used and it wasn't long until W. B. Morrison and R. S. Lazenby began bottling Dr Pepper. Soon there was a dearth of glass bottles ranging in style, shape and size. The history of carbonated beverage containers follows an evolution of ideas conceived by ingenious men dating back when it was first discovered how to capture and hold the effervescence of carbonated water.

The photo montage of Dr Pepper containers graphically illustrates the wide variety of packaging available in the 100th year of the Company's history.

At the beginning bottle shapes and sizes varied widely, some unique and odd in appearance. From early 1900 up until the late twenties there was constant change in packaging. By the twenties and up until 1950, package shapes and sizes were fairly consistent, most brands being served in 6 to 8 ounce bottles. Labeling on the first bottles was done with embossed lettering, a process that was used up until around 1950 when new products began to burst on the scene and the soft drink packaging revolution began. The first wave of activity came when major producers started introducing diet versions of their flagship brand. In 1962 Dr Pepper entered the parade with its low calorie sugarless drink labeled "Dietetic Dr Pepper."

The drink itself met with excellent results but its name did not.

Somehow it suggested that the drink was primarily for diabetics who necessarily restricted their intake of sugar.

Dietetic Dr Pepper was advertised for anyone, not just those concerned with a weight or health problem but who simply preferred it because of its taste which many did. To solve the name problem, the Company changed it to "Diet Dr Pepper" and immediately it caught the appeal of growing numbers of diet conscious consumers.

By 1963, one year after the initial introduction of Diet Dr Pepper, its taste had become the favorite of thousands of drinkers and the leading diet soft drink on the market.

The introduction of diet products had a profound effect, not only on soft drink packaging but they launched a barrage of other new versions of brand name drinks. In 1971 the Dr Pepper Company changed the name of its diet drink to Sugar Free Dr Pepper with a reformulated taste that won even greater consumer acceptance and became widely acclaimed as the No. 1 tasting diet soft drink.

Sugar Free Dr Pepper, however, would soon be joined by another diet Dr Pepper product that excluded caffeine. In view of the growing concern among some consumers about the effects of caffeine, it was inevitable that caffeine free drinks would appear, even though major studies did not confirm any harmful effects from caffeine.

It was no secret that each of the major soft drink producers had been experimenting with caffeine-free formulations. 7-Up was probably responsible for the accelerated activity in this area since

VIM
VIGOR
VITALITY
SATISFACTION
IN EVERY GLASS

5 CENTS
AT FOUNTAINS

DRINK
Dr. Pepper
— TRADE MARK —
KING OF BEVERAGES
FREE FROM CAFFEINE

Offering "Vim, Vigor, Vitality and Satisfaction," what more could one expect from a carbonated soft drink, plus the fact that it was "Free From Caffeine," as advertised by Dr Pepper in 1885.

In 1985 Dr Pepper still offers consumers plenty of reasons for drinking the product and a variety of package shapes and sizes; also a version of the drink that is "Free From Caffeine" and sugar as well.

85

it had launched a major campaign in 1982 assuring consumers there was no caffeine in their drink.

Dr Pepper Company had long since completed its research with its caffeine-free drink and on November 17, 1982 at a meeting of Dr Pepper bottlers in Houston, Texas, announced its new "Pepper-Free Dr Pepper" which not only was free from sugar but caffeine as well. It was the first decaffeinated sugarless Pepper-type soft drink on the market.

Initial distribution of the new Pepper-Free Dr Pepper began on January 1, 1983 in sixty selected markets in Texas, Oklahoma, Kansas, California, Arizona and Nevada.

Packaging for Pepper Free included 10 and 16 ounce PlastaShield glass bottles, 2-liter plastic bottles and 12-ounce aluminum cans. Graphics on the new package, designed by Alan Berni Corp., of Greenwich, Conn., featured a new color scheme of silver, red and blue, the latter color to identify with the predominantly blue Sugar-Free Dr Pepper packaging.

It is noteworthy that the original Dr Pepper, first introduced in 1885, was caffeine free and for many years this fact was exploited in its advertising. R. S. Lazenby, the man who perfected the Dr Pepper formula, was adamant in his claims that Dr Pepper was "Free from Caffeine." (See advertisement page 24.)

Much of Dr Pepper's early advertising stressed the absence of caffeine and some made disparaging comments about its harmful effects. It was not until 1917 that Lazenby had a change of heart when he discovered that caffeine was indeed a natural product.

The packaging parade among soft drinks has ballooned into gigantic proportions, much of it due to the proliferation of diet drinks. To satisfy the consumer however, producers have engaged in a competitive race to measure out drinks in greater quantity, all the way from 6 1/2 ounce to 3 and 4 liter bottles. Containers include glass, metal and plastic with paperboard now in the testing stage.

Dr Pepper is available in four different versions and in 46 varying size and type containers. The challenge to give the consumer the widest choice possible dominates the production and marketing of all brands. This, in itself, amounts to a herculean task for each manufacturer, not to mention the fight for shelf and display space in retail sales outlets.

One of the important developments which has brought greater emphasis on soft drink packaging is the loss of advertising space at the point of sale. For years bottlers spent enormous sums of money and produced great quantities of attractive advertising for display in retail outlets. Food store marketing, however, turned into giant supermarkets which offered little if any space for point-of-sale advertising. Thus packaging became the primary point-of-sale advertising vehicle.

The tremendous developments in the marketing of soft drinks within the decade '75/'85 are sure predictions of what lies ahead and they promise that the parade of packaging among soft drinks will continue for years to come.

A long established marketing strategy for Dr Pepper has been to make the drink available to consumers at the right place, in the right amount, at the right time and in the right form for maximum results.

"HORSEPOWER" DELIVERY _____

The history of product delivery of soft drinks has played a major role in their progress. It started when "horse power" was the four-legged variety and the primary mover of product. As late as the early twenties horse drawn vehicles were still widely used. The first motorized units were sometimes undependable but, as they improved, soon replaced the horse drawn equipment. Although the original delivery vehicles are in great contrast with today's modern variety, "horse power" is still the measurement of their load capacity. Delivery equipment has become far more than just a means for getting soft drinks into the market. It is a major advertising medium that gains the attention of consumers and literally serves as moving billboards. Their size and colorful graphics are impressive and offer unusual promotional value.

'85 WAS A VERY GOOD YEAR
... for America ... for Dr Pepper!

For Dr Pepper, 1885 was a very good year! It was good because it was a year of peace and calm with no great political, social or economic upheavals to cloud the scene. It was good also that the patrons of a small drug store fountain in Waco, Texas would enthusiastically approve this uniquely different tasting soft drink that was particularly pleasing to their palates.

It was a year of noteworthy events around the country and the beginning for some of the nation's leading products and companies. America's attention was focused on its western frontier and there was great anticipation about its future.

Many new companies and products were appearing on the scene during the mid-eighties to mark the beginning of the great industrial revolution that would soon create an enormous increase in production of many new goods and services. Today most historians agree that the Industrial Revolution was the turning point in the history of the Western World changing it from a rural and agricultural society to basically urban and industrial.

Texas, long noted as the second largest state in the Union (only Alaska is larger), came into distinction with its giant acreage ranches, one of the most famous being the XIT founded in 1885 by Taylor-Babcock Co., an English based firm. Located along the western border of the Texas Panhandle, it comprised nine counties and 3,500,000 acres. Its owners were granted the land in exchange for construction of the State Capitol building in Austin which was completed in 1888.

Two of the most celebrated landmarks in America, the Washington Monument, 585 feet high costing $1.3 million; and the Statue of Liberty were completed in 1885. Both are worldwide symbols of freedom which have inspired and given hope to people of every race and nationality.

The Statue of Liberty, a gift from France to the United States, was originally designed by Frederick Bartholdi. It has stood majestically in New York Harbor to welcome millions who have emigrated to America from every country in the world.

Grover Cleveland was inaugurated as the 22nd United States President in 1885 at the age of 47 and Mark Twain, the great American humorist, published his classic novel "Huckleberry Finn."

George Eastman, founder of Eastman Kodak Company (1880) revolutionized photography in 1885 when he introduced roll film which used a paper base instead of glass.

Annie Oakley became the legendary markswoman in America and joined Buffalo Bill's Wild West Show.

Gottlieb Daimler and Karl Benz, German inventors, developed the first combustion engine light enough to power an automobile in 1885. Daimler and Benz formed the company which produced the Mercedes Benz, the classic car of its time.

John M. Fox of Philadelphia learned about golf on a visit to Scotland and introduced the game in America. Considering the impact of the Daimler-Benz invention and the game of golf introduced by Fox, life in these United States has become completely mobilized and sports motivated in the 100 years that followed.

Henry Lee Higginson made music history in America on July 11, 1885 when he founded the "Boston Pops" orchestra. He had founded the Boston Symphony Orchestra in 1881 and his lighter form of music by a symphony group has become increasingly popular over the past 100 years.

Pasteur administered the first successful rabies vaccination in 1885 and the Exchange Buffet, first self-serve restaurant at 7th and New Streets in New York City, opened on September 4.

It was a birthdate year for a number of American companies. Good Housekeeping Magazine published its first issue in that year as did two leading Texas newspapers, The Dallas Morning News and The Houston Post.

Albert M. Butz of Minneapolis filed for a patent on his "damper flapper" in 1885 and Honeywell's first regulator came on the market. The company started when Butz and a group of investors formed Thermo-Electric Regulator Company, today known as Honeywell and the temperature in America has been under control ever since.

It was St. Louis in 1885 when William Seward Burroughs filed his patent application for his automatic adding machine. His first proved a failure as did the second, but the third worked and a great product and company came into being. Starting out as the American Arithometer Company, obviously to identify with the science of arithmetics, its name was later changed to Burroughs in honor of the inventor.

It was not, however, a very good year for all of America in 1885; particularly for the coastal city of Galveston, Texas where a devastating fire virtually destroyed the city leaving 5,000 families homeless and resulting in $2 million damage. Ironically, tragedy struck Galveston a second time only five years later when a giant tidal wave inundated the island city taking six thousand lives.

On a brighter side and more positive note, other 1885 happenings in Texas were more favorable. In Waco the new carbonated soft drink named Dr Pepper being served at Morrison's Old Corner Drug Store was gaining in popularity. From the beginning it had become a favorite among fountain patrons. Its origin is well documented elsewhere in this book but details of its progress are couched in numerous related stories.

Huck Finn was the loveable urchin in Mark Twain's great American novel "Huckleberry Finn" published in 1885.

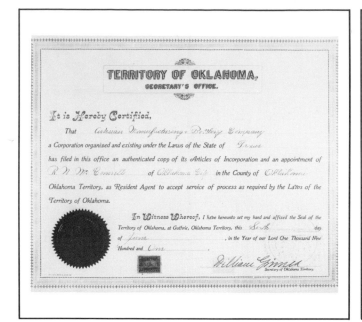

The Artesian Manufacturing & Bottling Company of Waco, Texas, fore-runner to Dr Pepper Company, was "authorized and licensed to do business" in the Oklahoma Territory on the 6th of June, 1901; and in the State of Missouri on the 13th of February, 1902. Original documents, officially signed and sealed, are preserved in the Dr Pepper archives.

Although Dr Pepper had its origin in Texas, records indicate that within a short time it had spread its distribution into Oklahoma and Missouri. In the Company's archives are two official documents, one from the State of Missouri and one from the Territory of Oklahoma, certifying that Dr Pepper was licensed to do business in each respective area.

The Missouri document, dated February 3, 1902, granted license to the Artesian Manufacturing & Bottling Company of Waco, Texas and was signed by Samuel B. Cook, Secretary of the State of Missouri.

The document from the Territory of Oklahoma was issued by William Grimes, Secretary, and dated June 6, 1901, likewise authorizing the Artesian Manufacturing & Bottling Company to sell Dr Pepper in the Territory.

The Artesian Manufacturing & Bottling Company was the fore-runner to Dr Pepper Company.

Dr Pepper advertising and distribution pioneered its way into many Oklahoma Territory outposts as early as 1901.

Eighteen eighty five proved to be a good threshold year for Dr Pepper as it soon found its way into many rural pioneer areas. In 1901, the year it was authorized for sale in the Oklahoma Territory, we find it being advertised and on sale in Ragtown, a mushroom camp made up of tents, covered wagons and various commercial shops on the outskirts of Anadarko. The Territorial government had scheduled an auction of 1,129 lots in the town of Anadarko and some 20,000 were on the scene to make bids. Once the auction was over, Ragtown disappeared overnight along with its migrant merchants.

Dr Pepper became a big favorite in the Oklahoma territory. A newspaper advertisement dated 1904 in the Moore, Oklahoma Enterprise featured "Dr Pepper — the Ideal Beverage."

J. T. and Lydia Newman were bottling Dr Pepper in 1908 in their plant in Pattonsburg, Missouri.

Situated between a laundry and a lemonade stand was this notions counter which sold Dr Pepper in Ragtown, Oklahoma in 1901. It was an overnight camp city made up of tents, covered wagons and make-shift merchant shops located on the outskirts of Anadarko, Oklahoma.

Over in Missouri J. T. and Lydia Newman were bottling Dr Pepper in 1908 in their plant in Pattonsburg, a community about 40 miles from Chillicothe. Pattonsburg is now serviced by the Dr Pepper Bottling Co., of Chillicothe, owned and operated by June Shaffer and his son W. L. "Butch" Shaffer, by no means newcomers to Dr Pepper having acquired the business in 1936 from J. L. Moyer.

Early scenes in Texas, Oklahoma and Missouri show Dr Pepper available in numerous remote areas. Needless to say few of the people in the photos can be identified but they help link Dr Pepper to its beginning.

These illustrations trace some of the early business developments of Dr Pepper throughout Texas and the Midwest. Both Oklahoma and Missouri were pivotal states in the migration to the West where pioneers were introduced to many new products.

This Dr Pepper advertisement appeared in the Moore (Oklahoma Territory) Enterprise on September 16, 1904. The reprint of the ad was furnished to Dr Pepper by John Womack of Noble, Oklahoma.

This photo was uncovered in an old picture frame in a Central Texas antique dealer's shop in the late thirties. It is reasonable to believe, from the facial expression on the gentleman on the left, that he had just enjoyed "Dr Pepper — King of Beverages." as advertised.

The Richie Post Office and Grocery Store in Richie, Texas, eight miles southwest of Waco, sold Tucker's Simple Remedies and Dr Pepper. It was operated by the Bullock Bros., and the picture was made in 1897.

The year 1885 was a very good year for America and for Dr Pepper for many reasons but most of all, because it was an exciting period in American history. As a part of that history it became a camp follower of the thousands who founded the West. Dr Pepper's founders were among the rugged individualists in the drama that began in 1885 and has continued through its 100 Original Years!

1885 was a fun year for this frolicking foursome of Waco belles who found the top deck of an Artesian Bottling Company delivery wagon a good place to have it. The two seated are Verna Campbell and Lena Gooch; standing are Edna Ard and Maude Billingsley.
The driver is Earnest Sparks.

Typical of the signs used to advertise Dr Pepper in early 1900, and most commonly seen, is the one pictured above.

DR PEPPER FOUNDERS
Perpetuated In Philanthropy

The founders of Dr Pepper Company perpetuated themselves through noteworthy endowments and philanthropic distribution of accumulated resources totaling more than $25 million. J. B. O'Hara, son-in-law of R. S. Lazenby who perfected the Dr Pepper formula and founded the Company in 1885, began the program prior to his death on December 30, 1961. His wife Virginia Lazenby, daughter of the founder, continued the process up until her death on April 15, 1975.

Virginia Lazenby O'Hara was responsible for carrying through with the program of philanthropy previously instituted by her husband. They had already made generous contributions to a number of schools and hospitals.

Mrs. O'Hara was graduated from Sweet Briar College in Virginia. During World War I, she met John B. O'Hara from Duryea, Pa., who was stationed in Waco, Texas for military training. Virginia Lazenby and J. B. O'Hara were married on June 19, 1919 at the close of the war.

O'Hara joined his father-in-law in his bottling works in Waco following his discharge from military service and ultimately became chairman and CEO of Dr Pepper Company. It was O'Hara who provided the management and marketing expertise that enabled Dr Pepper to become recognized as one of the leading soft drinks on the market.

Mrs. O'Hara's father died April 17, 1941. Mr. O'Hara assumed full responsibility for operating the Company and became recognized as a key industrial figure nationally. During his illustrious and colorful career he established Dr Pepper as one of the nation's top ranked soft drink companies.